MEGA
FUN
and
FACT
BOOK

Contents

These books first published 1985 by Octopus Books
Limited as The Mega Fun Book and The Mega Fact Book.
This compilation first published 1993 by Dean, an imprint
of Reed Children's Books, Michelin House, 81 Fulham
Road, London SW3 6RB
and Auckland, Melbourne, Singapore and Toronto.

Reprinted 1993

ISBN 0 603 55112 2

Printed in Great Britain by The Bath Press

MEGA

FUN and FACT BOOK

THE MEGA FACT BOOK
COMPILED BY **BRUCE MITCHELL**

THE MEGA FUN BOOK
DEVISED AND COMPILED BY **KATE MARLOW**

ILLUSTRATED BY **KIM BLUNDELL**

DEAN

THE MEGA FACT BOOK

IN THE BEGINNING

A romantic feast

In the mid-seventeenth century a Lincolnshire man kissed his wife in public. He was put in the stocks for two hours, because it was strictly forbidden to do such a thing on a Sunday.

Never on a Sunday..........

Open wide

The first dentists in America had to leave the country in a hurry. They filled teeth without taking away all the decayed parts, and their patients still got toothache. Until special schools were started in the nineteenth century, anyone could be a dentist. The record tooth puller today is an Italian. In 36 years he's pulled out two million teeth.

If the shoe fits

The first shoes were exactly the same for right and left feet. It wasn't until 1818 that paired shoes were made.

Umbrellas in the sunshine

The first people to carry umbrellas weren't sheltering from the rain; they were trying to keep out of the sun. The word comes from the Latin *umbra* which means shade.

Who was to blame?

The first two cars driven in Redruth in Cornwall crashed into each other.

One across

The Daily Express was the first British newspaper to print a crossword – on November 2, 1924.

The first Christmas card

In 1843 Sir Henry Cole wanted to send some
friends a message to wish them a happy
Christmas. He hired an artist to draw a picture
of a large family sitting round a table enjoying a
meal. This was the very first Christmas card.
Now billions of them are sent each year.

Zippers on the feet

*Whitcomb Judson of Chicago got so
tired of lacing up his boots that in 1893
he thought out a better way of fastening
them – the zip. At first it was the boots
and not the fasteners that were called
zips.*

A worthwhile dream

*The first thing Robert Louis Stevenson did when
he woke up one morning was to begin writing
Dr Jekyll and Mr Hyde. He'd dreamt the plot the
night before.*

Early recording

The first words that Thomas Edison spoke into
the recording machine he invented were 'Mary
had a little lamb.'

Not tonight Napoleon
The first time Napoleon tried to kiss his wife, Josephine, after their wedding, her dog bit him.

First things first
Among the first things to be loaded onto the QE2 when she joined the task force that sailed to the Falkland Islands in 1982 were three million Mars bars.

TRANSPORT

Walking tall

In 1891 Sylvain Dornon walked on stilts from Paris to Moscow (a distance of 1,800 kilometres – 1,125 miles).

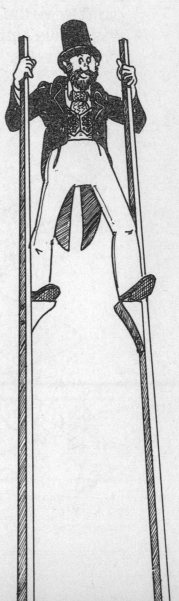

What's the busiest airport?

Every 52.2 seconds round the clock, every day of the year, a plane takes off or lands at Chicago's O'Hare International Airport.

When was the first supersonic flight?

The first time a manned aircraft flew faster than sound was on October 14, 1947, when Charles Yeager of the USAF reached 1072 kilometres per hour (670 mph) in a Bell XS-1 rocket-propelled research aircraft.

9

Who was the first man to fly a powered aeroplane?

Orville Wright. He tossed a coin with his brother to decide who should take their plane up first. Wilbur won, but the plane didn't leave the ground. The next day it was Orville's turn, and he took to the air for 12 seconds.

A life-like likeness

The Duke of Monmouth's first and only portrait was painted after he had been executed. His head was sewn back on; then the artist got to work.

The first balloon

Jacques Montgolfier was watching his wife hang her petticoat out to dry over a small fire when he saw it begin to rise in the air. This gave him the idea of making a hot air balloon.

Kickskull

The first football game is said to have been played in the 11th century when English workers dug up a Danish skull and began to kick it around between them.

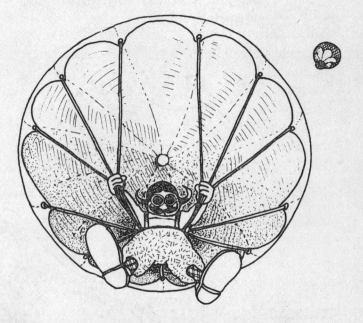

When was the parachute first used?

On October 22, 1797, André Jacques Garnerin was carried to 914 metres (3,000 feet) by balloon. He floated down to the ground again by parachute.

What was the largest car?

A Cadillac specially built for King Khalid of Saudi Arabia in 1975 was 7.6 metres (25 feet) long, and weighed 3,545 kilograms (7,800 pounds).

Who was the first man to fly?

It was Sir George Cayley's coachman, in 1809. Sir George had designed and built a glider, but was too old to fly it himself. He ordered his servant to take the machine up. The man did so, glided for a few hundred yards and landed safely. Then he resigned.

Gee-up...cats

In 1910 the eccentric Princess Radziwill of Poland rode in a chariot pulled by a lion and a leopard! She thought they'd be faster than horses. They weren't.

What was the largest passenger ship?

The HMS Queen Elizabeth. She was 314 metres (1,031 feet) long with a breadth of 36 metres (118 feet). During the Second World War she was used as a troop ship. She went up in flames in 1972 when she was being used as a floating university in Hong Kong.

The jinxed car

On June 28, 1914, Archduke Franz Ferdinand of Austria and his wife were shot and killed in their car. In the following 12 years, the car had 15 different owners and was involved in six serious accidents. Thirteen people were killed in it and many more injured.

CRIMES AND CRIMINALS

Timely Catch
A West German shoplifter shinned down a drainpipe to escape police. He then climbed over a high wall and leapt into the yard below. Unfortunately it was the yard of Dusseldorf Jail. Warders found stolen watches in his pockets, and he ended up doing time.

Letter Catch
Gunman, William Lindley, robbed a bank in Lithia Springs, Georgia, USA. He handed the cashier a note demanding money, but he made one mistake. The note was written on an envelope – and the envelope had his name and address written on it!

Meter Muck-up
Patrick Maxwell of County Tyrone, Northern Ireland was fined £25 in 1982 for fiddling his electricity meter. His crime came to light because he had blundered. He had adjusted the meter the wrong way and given himself a bill of £600!

Crime doesn't pay

A Frenchman murdered his uncle and then forged his will, making himself the sole heir. Unfortunately for the murderer, it turned out that the old man had been illiterate and that his housekeeper had written all his letters for 50 years.

A cool criminal

A woman in Nuremberg, Germany, passed out at the supermarket checkout. Staff took her large hat off as they tried to revive her and discovered a frozen chicken!

Escape into Captivity

Fifty prisoners in a Mexican jail decided to escape. They planned everything down to the last detail and then began digging an escape tunnel. When the tunnel was finished, they scrambled down into it and came up in the courtroom where they had been sentenced!

Home please, driver
An Indianapolis gunman was arrested after he held up a car, made the driver hand over his wallet, and then ordered his victim to take him home.

No fingerprints but...

A Tennessee burglar forgot his gloves one night. To avoid detection he took off his shoes and socks and used the socks as gloves. There were no fingerprints, but his footprints gave him away.

1. Which country has the highest murder rate?
Mexico – with 46.3 murders for every 100,000 of the population.

2. Which robbery got the most?
In 1979, three men were arrested after stealing 400 million dollars in cash, cheques and bonds.

3. The greatest jewel robbery?
When Prince Abdel Aziz Bin Ahmed Al-Thank's villa near Cannes in the south of France was robbed, thieves got away with gems worth over £7 million.

4. The largest ransom paid?
Over 25 million pounds was paid for the release of two brothers, Jorge and Juan Born in Buenos Aires, Argentina in June, 1970.

5. The most common international crime is
drugs smuggling. The second is art theft!

If the cap fits

A young husband in Florida was arrested for assaulting his wife. He said he was angry with her because she had hidden the caps of his toy pistol.

Fingerprints...

... were first used to convict a criminal in 1902. Harry Jackson was sent to prison for stealing billiard balls from a house in London.

The wrong note

A would-be bank robber in California pointed his pistol at the teller and gave her a note demanding all the money in her till. At least that's what he thought he had

given her. In fact, he handed over the shopping list his wife had prepared: 'Milk, bread, ... pick up laundry.' The girl burst out laughing as the robber ran from the bank.

Kings and Queens

The stamp of a good king

George V was a great stamp collector. During his life he filled 325 albums with some of the most valuable stamps. His own face was on quite a few of them!

He died on his birthday

King Harold of England was killed on his birthday in 1066 at the Battle of Hastings.

Which queen was said to be a witch?

Anne Boleyn. She was born with six fingers on one hand – a sure sign to people of Tudor times that she was a witch.

Who was King Bokodo?

He ruled the Congo for a few years during the last century – and stayed king for three years after his death. He decreed that after death his body should be wheeled around in its coffin, and that he should continue to be king until he decided whether to stay dead or not. For three years his subjects regarded him as their monarch until they eventually decided that he had made up his mind.

Bathtime

Queen Elizabeth I was considered exceptionally clean by her courtiers because she took a bath once a month. Louis XIV of France bathed only once a year and Louis XIII had five baths in his entire life…and he lived to be 42.

Which king...

Was the smallest?
Charles I was just 1.4 metres (4 feet 9 inches) tall.

Had the longest reign?
Pepi II, a sixth dynasty king of ancient Egypt inherited the throne when he was six years old. He died, still pharoah, 94 years later.

Had the shortest reign?
King Virabahu of Ceylon was crowned in 1196. He was assassinated a few hours later.

Weighed the most?
King Taufa'ahau of Tonga tipped the scales at 209.5 kg (462 lbs) when he was weighed in 1976.

Was the richest?
The oil-rich Amir of Kuwait had an income of £2.6 million pounds every week. That's about £15,000 a minute.

Was the last British warrior king?
George II became the last British monarch to lead his troops into battle, at Dettingen in 1743.

FOOD

A lot bigger
Popped popcorn is 20 times bigger than it is when uncooked.

Stale bread
A 3,500-year-old loaf of bread was found in an Egyptian tomb.

Beware
Only qualified and licensed chefs in Japan can cook fu-gu fish. If you don't cook it in the right way it is deadly poisonous. Every year approximately 200 people die because they try to cook it themselves.

When was the first fish and chip shop opened?
In London in 1865, when fish cost 1p a portion. Today, there are approximately 12,000 of them.

Deep frozen meat
When woolly mammoths were found perfectly preserved in the ice where they had lain for 50,000 years, some of the meat was thawed, cooked, and fed to dogs. They lapped it up.

The first ice cream...

...was brought into Europe by Marco Polo, a famous Italian traveller, in the thirteenth century. It was served at Henry V's coronation banquet in 1413.

Chewing gum...

...was invented by Thomas Adams, who originally thought it should be used as a substitute for rubber.

Big Mac

If all the MacDonald's hamburgers sold so far in America were piled on top of each other, there would be 20 piles as high as the tallest building in the world.

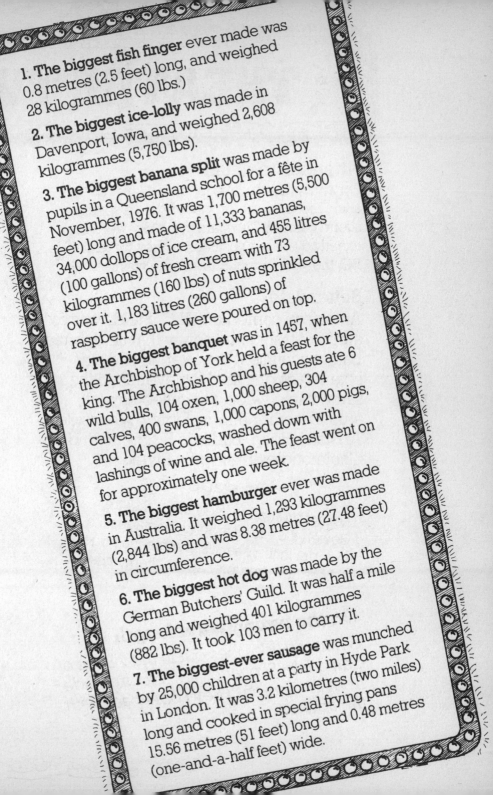

1. **The biggest fish finger** ever made was 0.8 metres (2.5 feet) long, and weighed 28 kilogrammes (60 lbs.)

2. **The biggest ice-lolly** was made in Davenport, Iowa, and weighed 2,608 kilogrammes (5,750 lbs).

3. **The biggest banana split** was made by pupils in a Queensland school for a fête in November, 1976. It was 1,700 metres (5,500 feet) long and made of 11,333 bananas, 34,000 dollops of ice cream, and 455 litres (100 gallons) of fresh cream with 73 kilogrammes (160 lbs) of nuts sprinkled over it. 1,183 litres (260 gallons) of raspberry sauce were poured on top.

4. **The biggest banquet** was in 1457, when the Archbishop of York held a feast for the king. The Archbishop and his guests ate 6 wild bulls, 104 oxen, 1,000 sheep, 304 calves, 400 swans, 1,000 capons, 2,000 pigs, and 104 peacocks, washed down with lashings of wine and ale. The feast went on for approximately one week.

5. **The biggest hamburger** ever was made in Australia. It weighed 1,293 kilogrammes (2,844 lbs) and was 8.38 metres (27.48 feet) in circumference.

6. **The biggest hot dog** was made by the German Butchers' Guild. It was half a mile long and weighed 401 kilogrammes (882 lbs). It took 103 men to carry it.

7. **The biggest-ever sausage** was munched by 25,000 children at a party in Hyde Park in London. It was 3.2 kilometres (two miles) long and cooked in special frying pans 15.56 metres (51 feet) long and 0.48 metres (one-and-a-half feet) wide.

THEATRE, TV,

Attention to detail

For a moonlight scene in the 1947 film *Caesar and Cleopatra*, the producers had a special scene painted. The stars in the sky were in exactly the same positions as they were in 46 BC, the year in which the scene was set.

Better safe

American comedian W.C. Fields was so afraid of losing his money that he opened bank accounts whenever he had any spare cash on him. He never used the same name twice. He called himself, amongst other things, Figley Whitesides, Aristotle Hoop, Ludovic Fishpond and Cholmondley Frampton Blythe.

On stage

The first prompters used in the theatre followed the actors around the stage with the script in their hands. If someone forgot his lines, the prompter spoke them himself.

On the wrong wavelength

When the tide goes out in the village of Carrodale, Scotland, T.V. pictures fade from the screen. They come back with the tide.

AND FILMS

A lot of letters
Charlie Chaplin, the famous comic actor, once received 73,000 letters in two days.

Poor old Dad
When one thousand children were asked, 'Which do you prefer, television or your father?' 440 of them said television.

The first moving picture...
...in America showed a man sneezing. It was filmed in 1894.

Which actress won the most Oscars?
Katherine Hepburn. She won her first in 1933 for a film called Morning Glory; *her second was in 1967 for* Guess Who's Coming to Dinner?; *her third in 1968 for* The Lion in Winter; *and her fourth for a film called* On Golden Pond, *in 1981.*

Why's an Oscar called an Oscar?
When the originator of the award first showed it to his secretary, she said, 'He's just like my Uncle Oscar.' The name stuck.

A long view
The average American 65-year-old has spent nine years watching television.

'A Good Time'...

... was the title of a play that opened in London in the 1900s. Next morning a journalist writing about the show wrote a simple one-word review: 'No.'

The long sleep

Andy Warhol's film Sleep lasts for eight hours. It shows a man sound asleep in bed – and nothing else.

She liked her coffin

Sarah Bernhardt, a famous French actress, was so fond of her coffin that she used to sleep in it occasionally. And five years before she died at the age of 78 she was still acting – despite the fact that she had a wooden leg.

Sport

The only truly American sport
Basketball is the only major international sport that is 100 percent American. It was invented by James Naismith at the YMCA training school at Springfield, Massachusetts, in 1891.

Where do people fly kites for sport?
Kite-flying is a major sport in Thailand, where they have kite-flying teams, umpires, official rules, and a national team championship.

Well watered
1,820,000 litres (400,000 gallons) of water are needed every year to keep all of Britain's golf course greens in trim.

That sinking feeling
Francis I of France was such a keen tennis player that he had a court built on his ship La Grande Française. Unfortunately the ship sank before the first game could be played.

Playing golf at the Savoy

International golfers staying at London's exclusive Savoy Hotel used to practise their drive from the hotel roof onto a barge in the nearby Thames.

Ten-ice

When the River Thames froze over in 1876, enthusiastic tennis players marked out a court on the ice and played on skates.

A new sport

A Yorkshire man went round England woggle-hopping. That's his word for leapfrogging over letter boxes.

Small competitors

At the 1904 Olympics in St Louis, two teams of pygmies took part.

Right on target

A Rhodesian (now Zimbabwe) archer scored a bull with his first arrow in a competition. His second one split it right down the middle of the shaft.

A cold race

Every year a sled-dog race is held in Alaska. The course takes 28 days to complete at temperatures of −62°C (−80°F).

And the winner is...

*The Emperor Nero entered the Olympics in
60 AD and won every event. His opponents
were so afraid of him that they always let him
win.*

Odd terms in tennis?

The word 'love' meaning 'no score' in a
tennis game comes from the French for
egg – l'oeuf. French scorers used to
draw an oval (or egg shape) on the score
sheet. 'Deuce', the word used when both
players have 40 points, comes from the
French à deux, meaning two to win.

Football Facts

1. Edward II banned the game of football in London in 1314 because it was interfering with archery practice.

2. When England won the World Cup in 1966 they almost didn't get a trophy: it was stolen from Central Hall in Westminster. Fortunately, just before the Tournament started, it was found by a mongrel dog called Pickles.

3. If a crowd of 100,000 football fans all cheered at the tops of their voices at exactly the same time, it would produce enough energy to boil three pints of water.

4. A Japanese footballer was so upset after scoring an own goal that he burnt his boots and became a monk.

5. All the members of an Argentinian soccer team were put in jail after a linesman was killed. He had indicated that one of them was offside!

The most runs from one ball

C.B. Fry, a well-known English cricketer, once hit a ball that landed in the fork of a tree. The umpire ruled that because it could still be seen it could not be counted as lost. Fry kept on running while the fielding side ran to get a ladder, and he scored 66 runs before the ball was retrieved.

A deep shot

During a cricket match at Eton, the ball landed in the path of a roller which squashed it into the ground. By the time it had been dug out, the batsman had scored 48 runs.

A hole in one hundred plus

A competitor in the Ladies Championship at Shawnee, Pennsylvania in 1912 took 166 strokes to sink her ball in the 16th hole. Many of the strokes were lost while she was standing in a rowing boat, trying to hit her ball as it floated down the river.

The moving turf

Every time Lord's cricket ground has moved location (three times so far) the original turf has been dug up and taken to the new site.

The long arm of the sportsman

Clifford Ray, a Californian basketball player, was called to a nearby zoo to help out in an emergency. A dolphin had a piece of metal stuck in its stomach and only Ray's arms were long enough to stretch down the animal's throat to get it out.

ANIMALS

Feeling slothful

It takes the sloth a week to digest a meal. This odd creature can also turn its head through a 270° angle. So although it spends most of the time hanging upside down looking upwards, it can see what's happening on the ground without moving too much.

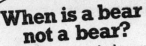

When is a bear not a bear?

When it is a koala bear. Koalas are related to the kangaroo.

A boring diet

The koala bear will only eat eucalyptus leaves – nothing else will do.

A fast youngster

A two day old gazelle can sprint at 96 km/h (60 mph) and outrun an adult racehorse.

Animal builders

In one night a beaver can use its razor sharp teeth to fell a 21-centimetre (6 inch) thick tree, cut it into neat logs and drag them to the riverside.

How does a bat know where it's going?

As it flies through the air it sends out a series of little cries. The sound waves bounce back off anything they hit and the bat knows where the object is.

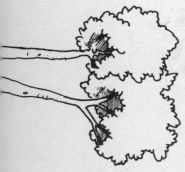

Small but deadly

The vicious wolverine weighs only 18 kilogrammes (40 lbs) but it can kill a caribou seven times its size. It can dig like a badger, climb like a squirrel, swim like an otter and jump high in the air. Fortunately it never attacks man.

Mass suicides

Whenever a lemming colony become too large, they leave their burrows and rush to the seashore where they jump into the water and drown. One Norwegian steamer took an hour to cut its way through water full of lemmings.

Food for the fish

A traveller in the Amazon valley was attacked by a swarm of wasps so he jumped into the river to get rid of them. Then he was eaten alive by piranha fish!

Which animal can kill a lion?

A small porcupine can kill a fully-grown lion. When the spiky creature is attacked it rolls itself into a ball. Any animal that tries to bite it gets a mouthful of quivers stuck in its throat, making it impossible for the animal to eat. It dies of starvation a few days later.

The walking vacuum cleaner

The ant eater doesn't have teeth or jaws. It catches ants on its long tongue and sucks them up through its snout. It may look quite a cuddly creature, but it has strong front feet with razor-sharp claws that can punch a hole in a man's chest!

Sweating blood

When a hippopotamus gets excited, its sweat becomes red.

Amazing dolphins

These clever animals have been known to support other injured dolphins until they can swim by themselves again. Dolphins also rescued a drowning South African girl; they have guided sailors away from rocks in a fog, and one badly cut dolphin swam close to a Russian fishing boat and lay perfectly still while the ship's surgeon stitched its wound.

Which animal has an inflatable nose?

The male sea elephant has a long nose that hangs down over its mouth. When it's angry it inflates its nose like a large balloon to show other animals that it is mad.

Quite foul

Hippopotamus meat tastes like old boots soaked in cod liver oil – no matter how it's cooked.

Never right

All polar bears are left-handed. They never use their right paws to attack or to defend themselves.

Film fan dogs

A film called *The Dog That Saved Hollywood* was first shown to an audience of 100 dogs.

Seasoned travellers

Dog owners in the Hague, Holland, can buy season tickets for their pets to travel on the city's buses and trams.

Clever dog

Film producer Mack Stennet had a dog called Teddy that could fill a kettle by itself.

Which animal is a farmer?

The aardvark always knows it will have enough of its favourite food, desert melons, to eat. When the animal drinks the water contained in the melon, it swallows the seeds as well. These are passed out of the aardvark in its dung, which it then buries. The seeds grow into new melons and the animal knows that if he goes back to the same spot some time later, there will be melons for it to eat.

Electronic sheep

Welsh farmers fit electronic bleeps to their sheep so that they can track them. The device is called Bangor Orange Position Estimating Equipment for Pastures – BO-PEEP for short!

Man eater

A leopard known as the Panawar man-eater ate over 400 people before it was shot dead.

Dog type

Arlecchino, a setter, was taught to use a typewriter. His owner built a special machine for him and he used his nose to punch the keys. He could type 20 words.

The camel...... can close its nose whenever there's a sandstorm.

The elephant...

...is the only animal with four knees.

Bearing the weight

The spine of one type of shrew is so strong that it can stand the weight of a human being on it.

The killer king

Henry III was a keen animal keeper. He had a zoological collection of monkeys, lions, camels and bears. But one day, for no apparent reason, he shot them all.

Spitting mad

When the llama gets angry it spits foul green juice with amazing accuracy.

PLANTS

Giant leaves

The leaves of the Brazilian palm tree are so long that if one of them were stood on end it would dwarf Marble Arch in London.

Slow growers

The giant cactus, saguaro, grows only 2.5 centimetres (one inch) a year. However it lives for so long it eventually reaches a height of 15.25 metres (50 feet) and weighs ten tonnes. It doesn't flower until it is over 50 years old.

The tree that isn't a tree

The banana tree isn't a tree at all – it's a herb. The trunks are huge stems and the bark is a hollow sheath of leaves.

Get planting

Since 1977 every person in the Philippines over the age of ten has had to plant a tree every five years. If they don't do so, they will be fined £150.

The tall krubi

The krubi plant that grows in Indonesia is taller than a man standing on another's shoulders. Also, it smells like rotten eggs.

Wed to a tree

In some parts of southern India, the youngest sons of a family cannot get married before the eldest. If the oldest brother has waited too long to find a suitable wife, he marries a tree so that his brothers can also marry.

Razor sharp grass

The Guaymi Indians never need to buy razor blades. The edges of the seeds of the grass that grows in parts of Panama are so sharp that they can be used for shaving.

Tree dwellers

The baobab tree has such an enormous trunk that it can be hollowed out and used as a place to live! One in South Africa is so big it has been used as a bus shelter.

Shaken to the roots
The colocasia plant has fits of shivering
that no one can explain.

Why are daisies called 'daisies'?
The word comes from two old English words
meaning 'day's eye'.

A square idea *An English gardener
has grown a
square tomato.*

A barren landscape
There are no trees at all in Iceland.

Named after a tree
The Brazil nut tree is not named after Brazil. The country is named after the tree.

Underground lighting
In some caves in Central Europe there are mosses which produce a green glow that is strong enough to light the way for pot-holers.

Fried or boiled?
More than two-thirds of the world's population lives on rice.

Can you eat seaweed?
Yes. In fact it's very good for you, since it's rich in iodine, which is vital for the human body.

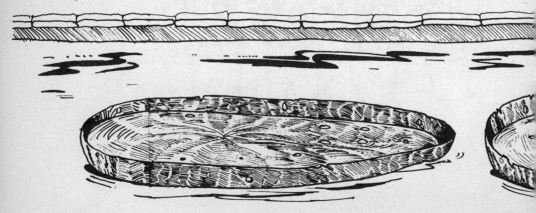

Which tree can defend itself?

The Mexican elephant tree sprays horrible-smelling oil if for any reason an animal attacks it.

Which water plant can support a man?

The pads of the Victorian water lily are so strong that they can take the weight of three men.

Soft wood

The inside of the baobab tree is so soft that a bullet can pass right through it.

Which plant smells like bad meat?

The carrion plant attracts carrion flies to it by its smell. The flies usually lay their eggs on rotting meat, but the plant imitates that smell and the fly is tricked.

Cold plants

The Arctic willow and the yellow poppy are the only plants to grow at 80°N in the Arctic Circle.

Guided by a plant

The compass plant is called that because the ends of its leaves always point north to south.

The cow dung plant!

The name 'cowslip' comes from an old English word *cuslyppe* which means cow dung, an odd name for such a sweet smelling plant.

The banyan tree...

... can grow to such a size and cover such a large area that Alexander the Great and his army of 7,000 sheltered under one!

Beware – leaf it alone

The stalk of the rhubarb plant is good to eat, but the leaf is highly poisonous.

The teazle merchant

The teazle is the only plant still used in exactly the same state as it is picked. The sharp hooks on its seed head are ideal for brushing the green cloth on snooker tables. The only surviving teazle merchant, in Huddersfield, England, handles 8 million a year.

Warming seed pods

The floss inside the seed pods of the kapok tree is used to fill sleeping bags and life jackets.

A proper corker

Cork trees have to be fifteen years old before their bark can be stripped.

Less iron than was thought

The idea that spinach contains more iron than any other plant came about when a scientist put the decimal point in the wrong place; he accidentally multiplied the real amount by ten.

INSECTS

Lots of ants
There are approximately one thousand billion ants living on the earth.

Wrongly accused
Moths don't eat the wool in your clothes. Their larvae do.

Efficient eyes
The dragonfly's eye has 28,000 lenses in it.

Losing their heads
Cockroaches can live for up to seven days after their heads have been cut off.

Stingless
Male bees (drones) cannot sting.

Killer bees

150 people in Brazil have been killed by bees. 500 stings are usually fatal but one man survived 2,243 of them.

Not red at all

An insect's blood has no colour. If you ever squash one and find red blood, it will be the blood of another animal that it's been feeding on.

Crawling with life

The Arctic may look desolate and lifeless, but more insects live there than mammals live in all of Europe.

More every year

Every year about 1,000 new species of insect are discovered.

There are more...

...insect species on Earth than all the other animal species put together.

The champion flea catcher...

...was a Chinese man who, in 1928, caught 21,000 of them in four hours.

Air conditioned hives
In summer, bees keep their hives cool by beating their wings – 200 times a second.

EAT AT
TOE'S
CAFÉ

If...

...a man could jump as powerfully as a flea, he could clear a 40-storey building quite easily.

Mother nature

During her lifetime, one queen termite can produce five hundred million young.

Well fed

One filling meal of human blood keeps a bedbug going for up to two weeks.

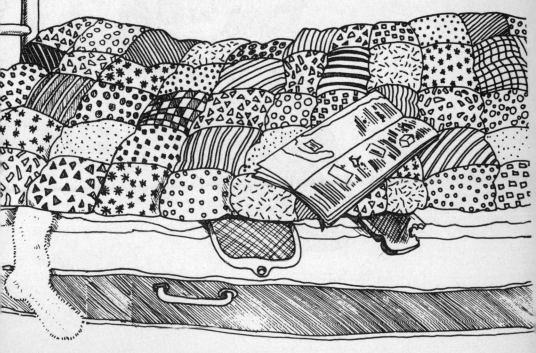

A lot of locusts

If all the locusts in a swarm 2 miles square were to breed successfully, in only four generations – just over a year – every bit of the earth's surface would be covered with them.

Banana peeler

The world's largest insect, the goliath beetle, can use its horns to peel bananas.

Lighthearted
Male glow-worms send out a flash of light every 5.8 seconds.

Fast flier
The hawk moth can fly at more than
53 km/h (33 mph).

Long in the body

*The female stick insect's body can
reach a length of 33 centimetres
(13 inches).*

If...

...every egg that every insect laid hatched,
then grew into an adult insect and lived its
natural life span, there would be very little room
for any other animal in the world.

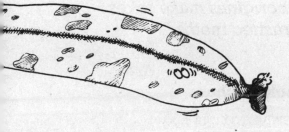

Killers
Mosquitos still infect over
40 million people with malaria
every year

A diet of insects
Australian aborigines make cakes from crushed moths.

Infested with cockroaches

Two Japanese housewives caught 1,300 cockroaches in their houses in one week. Their local supermarket had offered three pence for every one caught in the town. They had to pay out almost £3,000 when 98,500 were caught.

Long lived
Some ticks have been known to live for up to 25 years.

Perfectly camouflaged
It's almost impossible to see a Ceylonese walking leaf insect when it's on a tree. Even when the wind is blowing, the insect moves in the same way as the rustling leaves.

The higher the temperature...
...the more times a minute a cricket chirps.

Hard workers
It takes one bee 35,000 trips from flower to hive to produce just half a kilogramme (one pound) of honey.

Beware of the female
Only the female mosquito bites.

BIRDS

Gliding wonders
Albatrosses, with their large wingspan, are the gliding champions of the bird world. They can soar through the air without moving their wings for up to twelve hours.

High as a bird
Swedish waxwings got drunk after feeding on some berries that had fermented during the mild winter. Those that were sober enough to fly kept bumping into each other.

Frozen birds
Grouse bury themselves into snowdrifts and stay there for several days to get out of freezing winds.

The turkey drop

In Arkansas, seventeen turkeys were dropped from an aeroplane every year. People on the ground waited for the birds to land, chased them and carried their prizes home for the pot. Animal lovers complained, so frozen birds with parachutes attached are now used instead.

Affectionate fliers
Courting birds kiss each other with their beaks.

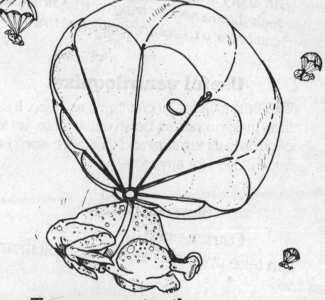

Temporary teeth

Baby birds in the egg have a special tooth that they use to crack the egg. It disappears shortly after they're hatched.

The swift......is the fastest of all birds. It can fly at 320 km/h (200 mph).

Covered talons

Boxing gloves came about from the leather coverings that fighting cocks used to wear before they went into the ring.

Going to work on an egg

Female ostriches crack open unhatched eggs and feed them to hatchlings that have emerged from eggs in the same clutch.

Powerful birds

An angry swan will attack a human being if it feels threatened. Its wings are so strong they can break a man's arms with one mighty flap.

Useful ventriloquism

The British Great Tit can throw its voice. It can then make intruders believe that there are lots of birds in its territory and that there won't be enough food for any more!

Slow on the boil

Ostrich eggs are so large it can take up to half an hour to boil them.

The kiss of life

When an Australian woman found an unconscious woodpecker in her garden she revived it with mouth to mouth resuscitation.

Nosey toucans

The toucan's beak is longer than its body.

Clever sewer

The male tailor bird makes his nest out of two leaves which he sews together with vegetable fibres. He punches holes along the edges with his sharp beak, then stitches and lines the nest with down.

Fast in the water *A Gentoo penguin can swim up to five times faster than the fastest human.*

The one-legged flamingo

When Pedro, a flamingo in a Norfolk Zoo, broke his leg, he was given a false leg made of plastic tubing.

Bird eyed

Birds have amazing sight but can hardly smell anything.

Caught by flying saucers

Basque hunters throw saucer shaped discs in front of flocks of pigeons. The birds mistake the saucers for hawks and dive to the ground for safety – only to end up in the hunters' nets.

Map shaped

Turkeys were given their name by English settlers in America because they thought the birds looked like a map of the country. (The Turks call them American Birds, because that's where they come from.)

In one piece

The secretary bird can swallow a hen's egg without breaking the shell.

Only the parrot…

…can move the upper and lower parts of its beak.

71

FISH

How does your garden grow?
The spider crab plants
seaweed on
its body as camouflage.

A little nipper
The pea crab is only six
millimetres (1/4 inch) long.

Quite a struggle
The largest fish caught
by rod and line was a five
metre (16 foot) white shark
weighing 1,208 kilogrammes
(2,658 pounds).

Which fish sings?
The scievia, a small Italian fish, sticks its head out of the water and sings.

A change of colour
Lobsters and crabs are blue in the sea. They only turn red when they're cooked.

Spitting champion
The archer fish from South-East Asia can dislodge an insect from a tree more than a metre away, by spitting at it.

Shocking

The electric catfish can kill prey with its 350 volt electric shock; the Nile fish uses electricity generated in its body to help it navigate.

Killer fish

An American hunter threw the carp he'd just caught on top of his shot gun. The wriggling fish got its tail caught up in the trigger... and the man was shot.

On...off

A small Atlantic fish can switch the light in its eyes on and off to attract food.

Danger from within

One Brazilian fish is so like another species that it can swim among shoals of its twin species unnoticed, eating one of them whenever it's hungry.

Odd ammunition

At the siege of La Rochelle in France, soldiers in the city ran out of cannon balls and began to throw oysters at their enemies.

A pearl of wisdom

It takes an oyster seven years to produce one medium sized pearl.

Well armed

Some starfish have as many as fifty arms.

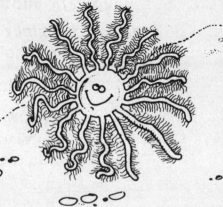

Picked clean
*Piranha fish have been
known to eat crocodiles
right down to the bone.*

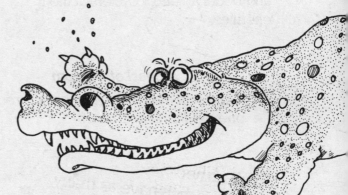

On the move
*Tuna fish die if they ever stop
swimming.*

Beware the stonefish
The spines of the ugly stonefish are so
strong they can pierce a thick rubber
sole. The poison they contain can kill a
man.

Guddling

Scottish school boys and girls often try to catch fish by tickling their undersides. The fish relax and are scooped out of the water. This is called guddling.

Big females, small males

The male angler fish is dwarfed by the female fish, which can be 50,000 times heavier than her mate.

Seasick

Fish kept in aquariums on ocean liners get seasick.

Not a bite

200 ambulance drivers held their annual fishing contest at a canal at Kidderminster. After five hours, not one fish had been caught. They learned that all the fish in the canal had been taken out and moved three weeks before!

Giant clams...

... can measure more than a metre and weigh 227 kilogrammes (500 pounds).

DINOSAURS AND REPTILES

Bird-sized
Some earth-bound dinosaurs were the size of a present-day chicken, and several of the flying dinosaurs were no bigger than a sparrow.

None across the water
There are no snakes at all in Ireland.

A harmless giant
The largest of all dinosaurs, the brachiosaurus, was a vegetarian.

A cool customer
A snake is a cold-blooded animal, which means that it can't adjust its body temperature. If the weather's too hot, snakes have to find shade or they'll boil. If it's too cold, they have to find warmth or they'll freeze to death.

Bird-brained
The stegosaurus weighed as much as 5,900 kilogrammes (13,000 pounds), but only 70 grammes (2.5 ounces) of that was brain.

Are all snakes poisonous?
No. Out of the 3,000 different kinds of snakes, only 250 are poisonous. Of these, only one – the adder – is found in Britain.

Shooting to kill
One type of African cobra attacks its prey by spitting poison at it. It's accurate and deadly: one squirt can blind a human.

Which is the longest snake?

It is the South American anaconda, which weighs 385 kilogrammes (950 pounds), and measures 11.5 metres (37.5 feet). It's a killer, and once it coils itself around its prey the poor animal hasn't got a chance. One brave adventurer wrestled with one for a bet, and won.

A glassy stare

Snakes have no eyelids.
Instead, each of their eyes is protected by a transparent covering, almost like a contact lens.

THE EARTH

How old is the earth?
Some rocks in Tanzania have been found to be three-and-a-half billion years old, but bits of meteors that have fallen to earth are a billion years older. So the earth is probably somewhere between three-and-a-half and four-and-a-half billion years old.

The hungry Falls
Since they were formed 10,000 years ago, the Niagara Falls have eaten their way 11 kilometres (7 miles) upstream.

If the earth were dry...
A man could walk around it non-stop, in a little over a year. A tidal wave would sweep round it in 60 hours, a bullet in 14 hours, and a beam of light in 0.1 seconds.

How deep is the ocean?
The Marianas Trench in the Pacific reaches a depth of 11,033 metres (36,188 feet).

Beware of quicksand
Quicksand is a mixture of sand and water on top of a clay base. The clay prevents the water draining away and the thick gooey sand sucks in anything unlucky enough to fall in!

The Great Wall of China...
...is the only man-made object that can be seen from space.

What's the highest mountain?
Mount Everest in the Himalayas at 8,846 metres (29,002 feet) is the highest peak in the world.

Where's it hottest...

The average temperature in

Dallul in Ethiopia is 34.4°C (94°F) but the highest temperature ever recorded was on September 13, 1922, at Al'Aziziya in Libya when the thermometer soared to 58°C (136.4°F).

Constant hot water

Old Faithful, the famous geyser in Yellowstone National Park, throws 33 million gallons of hot water into the air every day. That's enough to provide for the needs of a city of 300,000 people.

If all the ice melted...

...the sea levels would rise by 56 metres (185 feet). London, Paris, New York and many of the other major cities in the world would be submerged.

...and coldest?

On August 26, 1960, at Vostok in Antarctica the temperature dropped to an all time low of −88.3°C (−126°F).

The tropical Antarctic

Fossils found in the Antarctic have proved that today's icy wilderness was once a tropical paradise covered with lush trees and plants.

Where can you eat on the water?

The Dead Sea on the border between Israel and Jordan is so salty that it's almost impossible for swimmers to dive underwater. Four Israelis once had lunch sitting on dining chairs around a table floating on the surface.

Deluged

If all the Earth's annual rainfall came down in one great shower, the world would be covered by a metre (3 feet) of water.

How much water is there in the world?

70 percent of the world's surface is covered with water. There's 362,587,000 square km (140 million square miles) of it, with an average depth of 3,538 metres (11,600 feet). If it were spread evenly over the planet, all the land would be covered by 3,050 metres (10,000 feet) of water – apart from a few mountain peaks.

MONSTERS

The yeti

Well known mountaineers, including Eric Shipton and Don Whillans, claim to have seen the Abominable Snowman in the Himalayas. Whillans came across some huge footprints one day, and that night he says he saw the ape-like monster moving through the snow.

Monstrous children

Two Indian girls, Kamala and Amala, were found in a wolf's den when they were eight and one-and-a-half. When captured they were wilder than the wolf, and would only eat raw vegetables. They refused to wear clothes, slept most of the day, and went on the prowl at night. When little Amala died a year later, Kamala howled like a wild dog. Kamala died eight years after that.

A human monster

When Mohammed, Sultan of Turkey, found out that one of his servants had eaten his watermelon, he was determined to find out which of them it was. None of them confessed, so he ordered his doctor to slit open the servants' stomachs to find melon seeds as evidence of the crime. None were found. Mohammed apologized to the dead bodies.

And another

Another Mohammed, the Third, killed his 19 brothers when he came to the throne to make sure that none of them would rebel against him.

The three legged man

Sicilian Francesco Lentini was born with an
extra leg which he could use to walk and
run. When he was fully grown his extra limb
was just 7.5 centimetres (3 inches) shorter
than the other two, but it still worked.

Bigfoot

On October 20, 1967, Roger Patterson
photographed a huge hairy creature in California.
Seven years later it was seen again in Oregon.
One man followed a trail of its footprints – 1,098 in
all, 44 centimetres (17.5 inches) long and 18
centimetres (7 inches) wide. He didn't find
anything, luckily!

The mer-monkey

Circus owner Phineas Barnum charged people 25
cents to see a mermaid. He later confessed that it
had been made by fixing the top part of a
monkey to the lower part of a fish.

THE HUMAN BODY AND HEALTH

Going, going

By the time we're 60, most of us have lost half our taste buds and a lot of our sense of smell.

Sharp eyed

On a clear dark night, most of us could see a match being struck 80 kilometres (50 miles) away (if it was on top of a hill).

Bloodless

The cornea of the eye is the only part of our body that has no blood supply.

Owl eyed

Given enough time to get used to the dark, most of us can see as well as an owl.

Tubed wonders

Each kidney has more than one million tubes, which would measure 64 kilometres (40 miles) if put end to end.

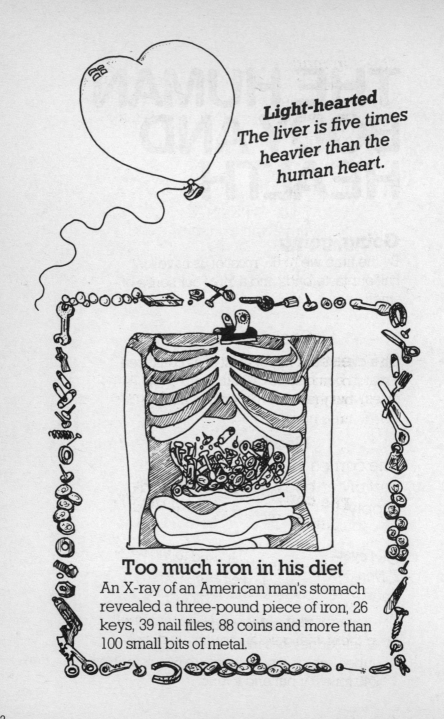

Light-hearted
The liver is five times heavier than the human heart.

Too much iron in his diet
An X-ray of an American man's stomach revealed a three-pound piece of iron, 26 keys, 39 nail files, 88 coins and more than 100 small bits of metal.

The thin man
From back to front, Claude Seurat's chest was only 7.5 centimetres (3 inches) thick. He made a fortune by showing himself off as the skinniest man who ever lived.

Not tongue tied
The tongue is
the only muscle
in the body
that's loose at
one end.

Tearless
Newly born babies don't cry! They can scream loudly but they can't shed tears until they're about three months old.

The commonest disease...
...in the world is tooth decay.

Flashing smiles
The Incas of Peru drilled holes in their teeth and filled them with gold and precious stones.

For a long life...

...move to Puerto Rico, where 21 percent of the men and 33 percent of the women live to be 85 or older.

Redheads...

...have fewer hairs than brunettes or blondes.

An odd toothache cure

People with toothache in the Middle Ages thought that if they ate a mouse, the pain would disappear.

Quite a head of hair

Swami Pandarasannadhi grew his hair until it was 813 centimetres (26 feet) long.

Uncut

A Shanghai priest didn't cut his nails for 27 years. They grew to more than 60 centimetres (24 inches) long.

Third time lucky
Some people have been known to grow three sets of teeth. Others never lose their baby teeth.

A tasty fact
There are 3,000 taste buds on your tongue but they can only recognize four tastes – sweet, sour, salt and bitter.

What an appetite!

Having eaten a splendid meal, Arpocras of Rome swallowed four tablecloths and a broken glass.

Hot footing it

An Indian called Kuda Bux walked over a bed of white-hot ashes at a temperature of 745°C (1,373°F). At times he sank in up to his knees, but doctors who examined him afterwards found no marks on his legs or feet.

A man of great determination

In 1978, Yukihiro Isa took five days to climb Mount Fuji. He's paralysed from the waist down and climbed the 3,778 metre (12,388 foot) mountain in his wheelchair.

His last chance

An American living in Maryland embezzled $30,000 from his employers when a doctor told him he had a few weeks left to live. He spent the lot and didn't die. A second opinion revealed that he had been allergic to the glove worn by the first doctor. He was given a suspended sentence.

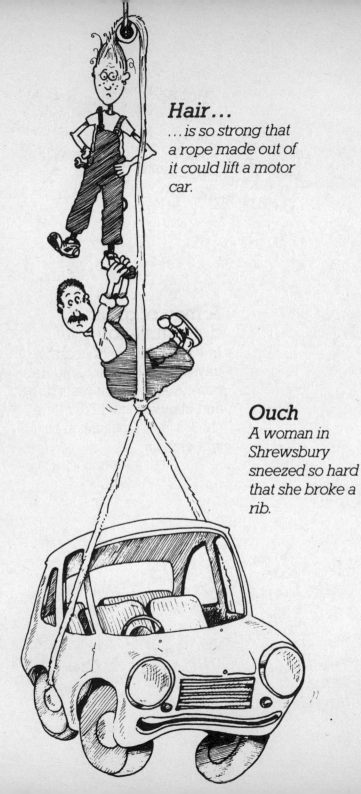

Hair...

...is so strong that a rope made out of it could lift a motor car.

Ouch

A woman in Shrewsbury sneezed so hard that she broke a rib.

Die...t

The author of a book called Nutrition and Health died because she didn't eat enough.

Toothless

Thirteen percent of the British population lose all their teeth before they're 21.

Yawn yawn

If you read the word 'yawn', the chances are you will.

Fingernails...

...grow at different rates. The one on the middle finger grows faster than the one on the thumb.

On the move

When we're asleep we change our position about 35 times.

SUPERNATURAL MYSTERIES

With her head on her knee

It is said that every May 19, Anne Boleyn's ghost drives up to her childhood home, Blickling Hall in Norfolk. The coach is drawn by four headless horses, and Anne rides along, with her head on her lap.

Killed by a ghost

In 1944, a motorist swerved to avoid an oncoming bus and was killed. But the bus wasn't really there – it's a phantom Number 7 that many Londoners have seen roaring through the streets with no driver at the wheel and no conductor to take the fares.

Seeing the point

Elias Howe, the inventor of the sewing machine, couldn't get his new creation to work until he dreamed that a tribe of cannibals had given him 24 hours to get it running. He noticed that their spears had holes at the point, and realized that a needle with a hole at the tip would solve his problem.

Up in smoke

Euphemia Johnson was having tea one afternoon when she burst into flames. She burned up, but her clothes were undamaged.

Haunted Britain

The United Kingdom has more ghosts reported per square kilometre than any other country in the world.

John Wesley's poltergeist

The founder of Methodism lived in a house in Lincolnshire that he shared with a ghost that knocked on walls, screamed during prayer meetings, dropped dishes, opened doors and tripped up visitors.

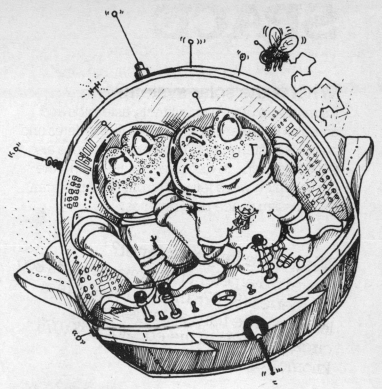

What was OFO-I?

In 1970, scientists were studying the effects of weightlessness on animals. Two male bullfrogs were sent into space in 1970, and the spaceship was called OFO-I. OFO stood for Orbiting Frog Otolith.

How hot is the sun?

At the centre, the sun's temperature is 15,000,000°C (27,000,000°F). It's much cooler at the surface – quite chilly in fact – only 2,482°C (4,500°F). It takes 8 minutes and 20 seconds for the light from the sun to reach the earth.

SPACE

What is the solar system?

It's made up of the sun, planets, asteroids and comets. There are nine planets, 48 satellites and countless asteroids and comets. There are also 4,000 bits of space debris zooming around the Earth, which were left over from the American and Russian space programmes.

What's the largest planet?

Jupiter's diameter at its equator is 142.800 kilometres (88,678 miles). The Earth is less than one third as large. Its circumference at the equator is 40,075 kilometres (24,900 miles).

Who was the first man in space?

The Russian astronaut Yuri Gagarin spent 108 minutes in space on April 12, 1961. Two years later another Russian, Valentina Tereshokova, became the first woman to travel in space.

What's the hottest planet?

The temperature on Venus has been measured at 482°C (900°F). It's the hottest of all the sun's planets although it's not the nearest. The reason? It's covered with dense cloud that won't allow heat to escape into space.

Blue moon

So much sulphur rose into the atmosphere after a forest fire in British Columbia in 1950 that the moon looked as if it were blue.

What's a comet?

A comet is made up of frozen gas and water, mixed with bits of metal and dust. The head is surrounded by a fuzzy cloud called a coma that can measure 1,610,000 kilometres (1,000,000 miles) across. The Star of Bethlehem, which guided the Three Wise Men to Bethlehem, may well have been Halley's comet. It completes its orbit every 76 years and can next be seen in 2062

How old is the moon?

Apollo astronauts brought back samples of moon rock that were estimated to be 4,720 million years old.

CLOTHES

Less than a tenth
A Texan ten-gallon hat only holds six pints of water (or, for the metrically minded: a 45 litre hat holds 3.4 litres!).

Leotards...
...were named after a French trapeze artist, Jules Leotard, who performed in specially-made one-piece elastic garments.

Quick change
One Austrian prince used to change his clothes as often as 30 times every day.

Smelly shirts
An American T-shirt maker sells T-shirts that smell. Customers have the choice of pine, orange, beer, banana, and twenty other aromas.

Not quite naked
An American shoemaker sells boots with pockets in them so that nudists can store things in them.

Rubbered out

In 1597, a young Spaniard returned home
from South America with a rubber cape.
He was tried for witchcraft because the
rain could not pass through his 'mac' and
was sentenced to death.

High-heeled Soles and heels on the shoes of Venetian women of the seventeenth century were so high that two men were needed, one for each arm, to make sure that the wearers didn't fall over.

Millinery

Hat makers are called milliners because the best hats used to come from Milan, Italy.

Mad as a hatter

Milliners used to treat felt hats with a mixture of mercury and nitrogen. Breathing those fumes can cause a disease called St. Vitus's Dance, which gives its victims delusions. This is where the expression 'mad as a hatter' comes from.

Knickers
One third of all the knickers worn in Britain are sold in Marks and Spencer.

BUILDINGS AND OTHER CONSTRUCTIONS

The pyramids...

...are the last of the Seven Wonders of the World still standing.

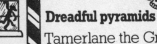

Dreadful pyramids

Tamerlane the Great, a 14th century Mogul chief, built pyramids out of the skulls of his enemies. The one in Isfahan was made from 70,000 skulls, another in Baghdad 90,000 and his biggest one, at Delhi, contained 100,000 skulls.

The largest pyramid...

...is not in Egypt, but in Mexico. The Quetzalcoatl is big enough to contain 40 football pitches.

New York's tallest buildings...

...are the twin towers of the World Trade Center. They are 412 metres (1,350 feet) high. Philippe Petit shot a tightrope between the two and walked half-way across it. Then he stopped and danced for 45 minutes.

Up in smoke

A cinema in California burned down just after the audience had seen a film called *The Towering Inferno*.

Running water in Rome

The Romans built an aqueduct system that carried 300 million gallons of fresh water into the city every day.

A river of concrete

When the Hoover Dam was being built in America, concrete had to be poured continually for two years.

Going going gong

The oldest gong clock in the world is in Notre Dame de Dijon Cathedral in France. It was made in 1383 and has struck more than 33 million times.

A strange conviction

Sarah Winchester believed that she would die if she ever stopped adding rooms to her house. 38 years, 160 rooms, 2,000 doors, 10,000 windows, 9 kitchens and £3.5 million later she stopped building and died.

Rooms to let

There are 1,400 rooms in the Vatican.

The Venice of the Midlands

 There are more miles of canals in Birmingham, England, than there are in Venice.

The White House...

...was the first building erected by the American Government. It wasn't called the White House until it was painted white to cover the damage caused when the British burned it in 1814.

The Statue of Liberty

The statue was a gift from the people of France; the Americans only paid for the granite and concrete pedestal.

With room to spare

Most of the cathedrals in the world could be fitted into St Peter's in Rome, with room to spare. St Peter's has 44 altars, 399 statues and a dome that could hold Buckingham Palace.

Bottled up

David Brown of British Columbia, Canada, made a house out of 500,000 bottles. Another man in the United States made his home out of used tin cans.

The prehistoric house

A shop in California is built like a dinosaur. The entrance is in the tail.

There's a tunnel under the London to Exeter motorway that's less than a foot wide – roadbuilders dug it so that badgers could cross the road safely.

The animal underpass

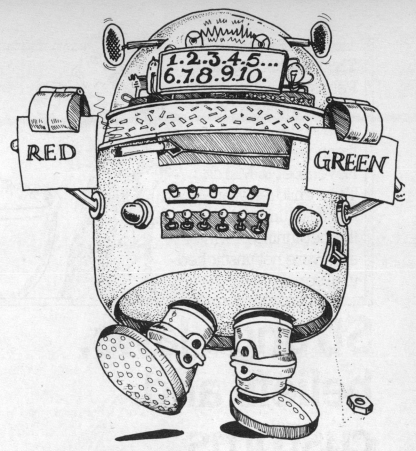

Man-made man

A robot called Elektro was built for the
World Fair in New York in 1939. It could
smoke, walk, count up to ten and
distinguish between red and green. Inside
there was enough wire to stretch right
round the world.

Standing in the corner

An Englishman hated women so much that he had
special holes cut in all the passages in his house.
His maids were under strict orders to hide
themselves inside these holes whenever they heard
their master approaching.

Thou shalt not bathe
Pennsylvanians tried to get a law passed in 1840 to stop people having a bath from November to March. Their children were sewn into their underclothes at the beginning of winter and were not unstitched until spring.

Strange laws, beliefs and customs

Champion flogger
In the days when it was legal for schoolchildren to be flogged by their teachers, one headmaster of Eton beat 70 boys in one thrashing. He hurt himself so badly that he was unable to move for a week.

The weight of the law
The Mayor of High Wycombe (or the Mayoress), along with the Deputy Mayor or Mayoress, Town Clerk, and Councillors is weighed every year to make sure that they haven't grown too fat while in office!

Thou shalt bathe

The men and women of Kentucky are quite clean. There's a law in that state that forces everyone to have a bath at least once a year.

Uniform hankies

Louis XVI decreed that all handkerchiefs should be the same shape.

A tasteless tie

A Polish man was fined for making his wife eat a tie she had given him as a present. He didn't like it.

Double file

A law in Toledo, Spain makes it illegal for pedestrians to walk on the pavement more than two abreast. Instant fines of 30p are imposed on law-breakers.

Growing on

Indian war heroes were buried in long tombs, since it was thought that if their fame grew after they died, so would their bodies.

If the hat fits

Kentucky wives must, by law, accompany their husbands when they go to choose a hat.

Playing cards...

...were once used as the official currency in Canada.

Ho-spit-ality

Masai tribesmen spit at each other when they meet and when they part. Newborn babies are spat on as a sign of good luck, and traders spit at customers when a bargain is sealed!

Not in public, ladies

New York women are banned from smoking in the street.

Mad measurement

In Peru a journey is measured not by the distance but by the number of cigarettes a traveller can smoke on the road.

BOOKS
AND
AUTHORS

A long run

J.M. Barrie's *Peter Pan* was written in 1904. It has been put on the stage every Christmas since then, except for 1940. Peter was always played by a girl until the Royal Shakespeare Company staged the play in 1982 – quite a twist, since in Shakespeare's day all the female parts were played by young boys!

On the up

Lewis Carroll wrote Alice's Adventures in Wonderland *standing up.*

The Wizard of Oz...

...is just one of fourteen Oz books written by L. Frank Baum.

Mark Twain...
... was the first author to use the newly-invented typewriter.

Safety first

The safety pin was invented in 1849. Walter Hunt needed $15 to pay off a debt, so he made the first one and sold the idea to a manufacturer for $15. It took him just three hours.

INVENTORS AND INVENTIONS

Who invented dynamite?

Alfred Nobel. He made so much money out of it that he left £1,750,000 when he died in 1896. The money is used to fund the Nobel Prizes, awarded every year to six outstanding men or women for physics, chemistry, medicine, literature, peace and, since 1969, for economics. The winners get £35,000 each.

Gerard Hale...

...invented the parking meter. They were first used in 1935 in Oklahoma. When the meters were put up in a town in Alabama a year later, the people chopped them down with axes.

The first fags

When their hookah pipe was destroyed by gunfire at the Battle of Acre in 1799, Turkish troops rolled their tobacco in the touch papers used for firing their cannons. And so cigarettes were invented!

Too lumpy

Hanson Gregory told his mother that her cakes were too lumpy in the middle. Mrs Gregory removed the centres and created doughnuts.

BOMB

Very polite

An Englishman made a top
hat that he could raise
whenever he passed a lady.
It was connected to a bulb in
his pocket by a rubber tube.
One squeeze of the bulb and the
hat tilted upwards. Two squeezes and
it was back in place.

SCIENCE AND SCIENTISTS

Revenge is sweet

A computer scientist programmed his computer so that if he were ever fired from his job, the computer would wait six months and then rub out everything stored in its memory. He was sacked, and six months later the company went bankrupt.

A deadly sip

Karl Scheele, a Swedish chemist, used to sniff and taste all the compounds he experimented with. He swallowed cyanide and survived, but died of mercury poisoning!

Big bang

An American scientist built the world's largest firework. It weighed 340 kilogrammes (748 pounds) and was 101 centimetres (40 inches) long. It was supposed to shoot up more than 1,000 metres (3,050 feet), explode and send a cascade of glittering sparks into the sky. When the fuse was lit, the rocket failed to leave the ground, and blew a huge hole in the earth instead.

Not a penny

Albert Sabin, whose anti-polio vaccine is widely used, refused to make any money out of it. He said he didn't want to profit from the health of men.

Albert Einstein

One of the greatest scientists of this century couldn't speak properly until he was nine years old. His work made possible the development of nuclear weapons. When the first A-bomb was exploded, Einstein said that if he had known what was going to happen, he would have been a plumber!

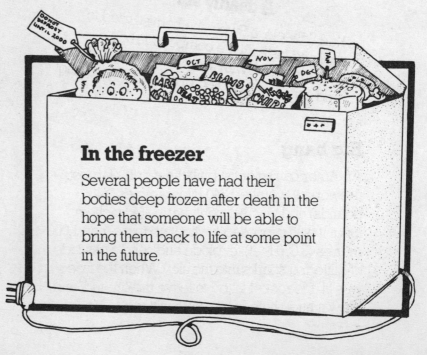

In the freezer

Several people have had their bodies deep frozen after death in the hope that someone will be able to bring them back to life at some point in the future.

Merchandise 7X...

...is so secret that the recipe for it is locked in a Georgia safe. Only a handful of people know the contents of the recipe -- it's the formula for Coca Cola.

Out cold

The first man to use ether to put a patient to sleep was an American dentist, William Morton, in 1846.

ALL SORTS

Hard to swallow

A man in San Antonio, Texas, has eaten 250 goldfish. Why? Because he likes them.

A change of career

Packy Ease did not have much luck as a boxer, so he changed his name and his job. Today he's better known as Bob Hope.

Safety first

One kind of bullet-proof vest can stop a bullet at point blank range, yet it only weighs one-and-a-half kilogrammes (three pounds).

Spacemen down under

Australian cave paintings dating from prehistoric times show men wearing garments which look very like space suits!

The sound of the sole

Japanese people used to select their wooden shoes not for their appearance but for the sound they made. It was bad taste to wear 'loud' footwear.

A sad loss

Among the oddest items handed in at the London Lost Property Office have been false teeth, a stuffed gorilla and an artificial hand.

A much married man

Brigham Young, the founder of the Mormon Church, had 27 wives and 56 children.

Square rings

Boxing platforms are called rings because in ancient Rome, boxers fought in round arenas.

The poisonous platypus

The oddest mammal in the world-with its webbed feet and strange snout-kills its prey with poison fangs.

129

Joan of Arc

After Joan of Arc was burned at the stake, her heart was found unburnt amongst the ashes.

Built on gold

The foundations of the Purandhar Gate near Puna in India are solid gold. There are 50,000 precious bricks under the ground worth, today, about 35 million pounds.

Mass wedding

1,800 couples got married in one huge wedding ceremony at Seoul in South Korea in 1975. They were all members of Sun Myung Moon's Unification Church.

Double bad luck

Several years ago, a Bermuda man was killed riding his moped down a street. He was involved in a crash with a taxi. Exactly a year later his brother was killed riding the same moped down the same street, by the same taxi, driven by the same driver, carrying the same passenger.

Wrong

'No woman in my lifetime will be Prime Minister.' The person who said that in 1969 was Margaret Thatcher, who went on to become Prime Minister.

Famous last words

'Die, my dear doctor, is the last thing I shall do,' said Prime Minister Lord Palmerston. A few moments later he did.

Pearly black

Chinese women used to dye their teeth black. They thought it was a sign of great beauty.

Instant tan

There's an American doll that gets a suntan if she's put under a lamp. An hour later the tan fades.

A bird's life

The oldest caged bird ever was a budgerigar called Joey. He lived to be 34 years old.

The valley of death

700 horsemen rode in the famous Charge of the Light Brigade. 505 were killed. The commander, Lord Cardigan, escaped.

One in the eye

Many people think that Lord Nelson lost his right eye after it had been shot out. It wasn't. A shot fired in his direction hit the ground in front of him, throwing up gravel into his face. It was the gravel that caused him to lose the sight of the eye.

That's their funeral

When the crew emerged from one of the first submarine dives in 1851 they had been down for seven-and-a-half hours. They came out of the ship and found a funeral service being held for them!

Famous last words

Beethoven's last words were 'I shall hear in heaven.' The famous composer had been completely deaf for eight years, during which time he had written some of his greatest music.

A hard struggle

Puzzled by logarithms? Don't despair! It took their creator, John Napier, twenty years to work them out.

Monkey business

In the film *Tarzan and the Apes*, all the monkeys were played by members of the same athletics club. The only real animal in the film was a lion – and it attacked the star, Elmo Lincoln.

Humble beginnings

Sean Connery, who shot to stardom as James Bond in Dr No, *used to be a milkman and a coffin polisher.*

Life saving president

Ronald Reagan, the 40th president of the United States, saved 77 people from drowning when he was a lifeguard in California.

A success story

Before he founded Marks and Spencer, Michael Marks used to peddle penny items from a tray round his neck.

Bad luck

A Belgian robber left a house with his booty, climbed over a wall at the bottom of the garden and found himself in Antwerp's prison exercise yard.

Once too often

After two years of constant hiccuping, Heinze Isecke found a cure for them. He threw himself out of a high window and killed himself.

It was in the cards

In the game of poker, two pairs, aces and eights, are the 'dead man's hand'. Wild Bill Hickock picked up such a hand and was shot in the back a few seconds later.

Almost two a minute

A car is stolen every 32 seconds in the United States.

Hard to kill

Many Russian noblemen resented the power that a humble monk, Rasputin, held over the Tsar and his family. They decided to kill him, but the poison they put in his food failed. So, too, did the four bullets they fired into him, and the many stab wounds they inflicted. They eventually drowned him in the River Neva.

Long distance emergency

A Leeds man was talking to his sister in Australia when the line suddenly went dead after the man had heard strange noises. He called his local police station. The officer on duty rang directory inquiries to get the number of the police station in Australia nearest to the man's sister. He then rang them. They rushed round to the woman's house to find her fighting off an attacker. It had taken just 18 minutes.

Snail's space

If all the snails eaten by Frenchmen every year were laid end to end, they would stretch round the world one-and-a-half times.

Not their own clothes

During the Second World War, 50,000 Allied officers hired their uniforms from Moss Bros.

Outerwear

French women of the fourteenth century used to wear their corsets on the outside.

The last wolf...

...seen wild in England was spotted in 1864. One village in Yorkshire still has an official wolfcatcher who is paid £2.00 a year.

An odd job

The ghost train owner in Brighton's pier employed a feather tickler. His job was to hide in the darkness and tickle passengers with a long feather to frighten them.

Greetings

As well as shaking hands when they meet, Tibetans bump foreheads. The Eskimos, as most people know, rub noses.

'What did you say?'

Captain Cook pointed at some strange animals he had never seen before and asked local Aborigines what they were. They replied 'kangaroo', but they weren't telling him the name of the animal. They were asking him what he had said!

Happy family

Siamese twins Chang and Eng married two sisters and had 21 children between them. The twins lived to the age of 63. For the last four years of his life, Chang was ill and had to stay in bed. Eng had no choice but to stay there too!

Fast work

Frank Richards, the author of the famous Billy Bunter stories, once wrote 16,000 words in one day. During his lifetime he wrote 60 million words – and he always wore a dressing gown, black skull cap and a pair of bicycle clips when he worked. He said the clips kept his legs warm.

Mark Twain

The author of Huckleberry Finn *and* Tom Sawyer *was born in 1835, a year when Halley's Comet flared across the sky. He always said that he would die when it next appeared in 1910. He did.*

A change of mind

Hans Christian Andersen went to live in Copenhagen to train to be a ballet dancer. Unfortunately he wasn't very good at it, so he turned to writing instead.

Early starter

Mozart had written fourteen operas by the time he was fifteen.

The curse of Tutankhamen

Members of the expedition that discovered the treasure of the Egyptian pharoah were warned that there was a curse on it. The man who financed the trip, Lord Carnarvon, was bitten by a mosquito and died a few days later when the bite went septic. At the exact moment of his death all the lights in Cairo went out for no reason at all. And thousands of miles away in England at the same second, the Earl's favourite dog howled and died.

Strange endings

A shock for the family
Henry Erskine went to answer a knock on the door one day in 1670 and was astonished to see his wife there. He'd just been to her funeral.

Suspended sentence
In England during the nineteenth century, anyone who attempted suicide and failed was liable to be hanged as punishment. Not for failing, but for trying to kill themselves in the first place.

Sewercide
*Two hundred sheep in Italy
jumped into a river.
No one knows why.*

A fatal note
Opera singer Leonard Warren had just sung the word 'fatal' when he died of a heart attack.

Generous to the end
A Frenchman walked into a hospital, signed over his body to medical research and committed suicide.

The death cards
Wild Bill Hickock, Al Jolson and Buster Keaton all died playing cards.

Killed by a monkey

King Alexander of Greece was bitten by his pet monkey in 1920. The wound would not heal and the king died of blood poisoning a few days later.

Drunk after his death

When King Mausolus died in 353 BC, his wife mixed his ashes with water and drank the lot.

The demon drink

3,000 Indians in New Delhi die every year from drinking home-made alcohol.

What a way to go

A Greek playwright, Aeschylus, was killed when a bird dropped a tortoise on him.

Still working

An American woman took her husband's ashes home, put them in her coffee grinder and put the fine powder in an egg timer.

Too good

Hungarian stag hunter, Endre Bascany, could imitate a stag's mating call so well that another hunter shot him.

Ouch

A 98-year-old Greek philosopher killed himself when he hurt his finger.

Killingly funny

A Greek playwright called Philemon thought one of his own jokes was so funny that he died laughing at it.

Dead and alive

Everyone thought Anna Bochinsky was dead, but as she was being carried to her funeral in an open coffin, she sat up and jumped out of it. Unfortunately she ran into the road and was knocked down and killed.

Drowning on dry land

An American woman ended it all by drinking so much water that she wasn't able to breathe.

A strange suicide

A French restaurant owner killed himself when a delivery of fish didn't arrive on time.

Hot tempered

Madame Lui, a French housewife, was murdered by her husband because she burned his toast.

THE MEGA FUN BOOK

DEVISED AND COMPILED BY **KATE MARLOW**

ILLUSTRATED BY **KIM BLUNDELL**

Contents

Mega words

A coded message

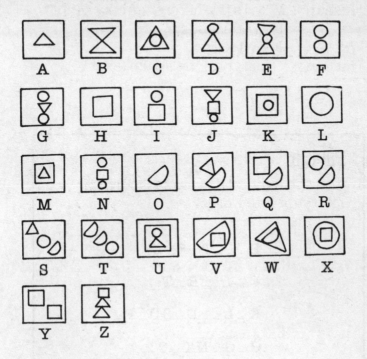

What is Zak's message?

Use this code to make up your own messages. Can you make up your own code?

Knock, knock.
Who's there?
Tim.
Tim who?
Tim-ber!

Brownie: Has your tent always leaked?
Scout: Oh, no! only when it rains!

Husband: What's the difference between a
taxi and a bus?
Wife: I don't know.
Husband: Great then, we'll take a bus!

Fill it in

Can you supply the vowels to turn the
following into words?

B _ _ _ T _ F _ L

F _ V _ _ R _ T _

K _ L _ _ D _ SC _ P _

G _ G _ NT _ C

S _ T _ SF _ CT _ RY

SP _ CT _ CL _ S

S _ CC _ SSF _ L

1st boy: Did you hear what happened to
the peanuts?
2nd boy: No, what?
1st boy: They were walking down the
street, and one of them was
assaulted!

Phrase phase

Can you unravel the mixed-up phrases?

Purr of a lion

Blast of an owl

Roar of a clock

Tick of a door

Slam of a turkey

Neigh of an explosion

Gobble of a kettle

Hoot of a horse

Crack of an engine

Whistle of a whip

Mega words

Word mad

By using the letters from one word you can often make a lot of new words.
For example,

MATERIAL

makes – TRAM, RAM, MAT, TAIL, TRAIL, MAIL, MALE, LAME, TAME, LATE, MATE, RATE, TEAR, LIAR, AIR, TERM, ALARM, RAT, LET, ART, and many more.

Can you do the same with these words?

DISAPPEAR   TELEVISION   RESTAURANT

INSTRUMENT

If you manage to use every single letter from the original word in your new word, it is called an anagram. They are often used as clues in cross-word puzzles.

Now try making new words using the letters in your own name.

For example,
BILLY T. O'SHEA
can be re-arranged as
LABEL HIS TOY

KAREN SIAM
becomes
MAKES RAIN

See what can happen to *your* name!

George: Dad, there's a man at the door with a bill.

Dad: Impossible! It must be a duck with a coat on.

Fill it in

Can you fill in each gap with the name of an animal, to complete a well-known saying?

1. A queer _ _ _ _
2. To have a _ _ _ in one's bonnet
3. It's raining _ _ _ _ and _ _ _ _
4. Smell a _ _ _
5. Let the _ _ _ out of the bag
6. Take the _ _ _ _ by the horns
7. Act the _ _ _ _
8. _ _ _ _ _ play
9. A fine kettle of _ _ _ _
10. As the _ _ _ _ flies
11. A _ _ _ on hot bricks
12. A _ _ _ _ ' _ eye view
13. Dead as a _ _ _ _
14. No _ _ _ _ _ on him
15. The _ _ _ _ ' _ share
16. A _ _ _ in the ointment
17. A _ _ _ in the manger
18. Stubborn as a _ _ _ _

Brainteaser

If three council workmen can dig five holes
in two days, how long would it take one
council workman to dig half a hole?

Captivating question

Maid Marion is looking for Robin Hood, who has been captured by King John.

She knows that Robin is inside one of these two cells, and that the executioner is in the other one.

Each door is carefully guarded. One guard ALWAYS tells the truth, and the other ALWAYS tells lies.

What is the one question Maid Marion must ask to find Robin Hood?

Customer: Waiter! Waiter! What's this maggot doing in my salad?

Waiter: Wriggling!

Q: What can you serve but never eat?
A: A tennis ball.

Q: What's big and white and can't climb trees?
A: A refrigerator!

Classroom chaos

The blackboard in class 3a is covered with a mumbo-jumbo of letters!

Use the letters to spell as many words as you can which read the same backwards or forwards. (These are called palindromes.)

For example: **dad, radar, level**.

Use as many letters as you like in each word, but only repeat a letter within a word if it is repeated on the blackboard.

Customer: Waiter, waiter! you've got your thumb in my coffee!

Waiter: Don't worry, sir: it isn't hot.

True or false?

1. Boys have more ribs than girls. True or false?
2. The capital of the United States is New York. True or false?
3. Alexander Fleming discovered penicillin. True or false?
4. A Palomino is a man from Sicily. True or false?
5. Bleriot was the first man to fly across the Atlantic Ocean. True or false?
6. Shirley Crabtree is a famous wrestler. True or false?
7. 150 is the highest possible score from three darts. True or false?
8. Origami is a herb which is used to flavour food. True or false?
9. Snowdon is the highest mountain in Britain. True or false?
10. Wellington boots were named after the Duke of Wellington. True or false?

1st Boy: What has eyes but no nose, a tongue but no teeth, and is a foot long?

2nd Boy: A shoe.

1st Boy: Bless you

1st Girl: Do you believe in free speech?

2nd Girl: Yes, of course.

1st Girl: Fine. Can I use your telephone?

Odd one out

Which is the odd-one-out in each of these groups?

1. CARROT, POTATO, CABBAGE, SWEDE, TURNIP
2. TIGER, HYENA, LION, LEOPARD, ZEBRA
3. SWAN, PIGEON, SEAGULL, DUCK, MOORHEN
4. APPLE, ORANGE, PINEAPPLE, PEAR, DATE
5. MANCHESTER, OSLO, PARIS, WASHINGTON, DUBLIN
6. WOOL, NYLON, SILK, COTTON, LINEN

Guest: Can you give me a single room and a bath?

Receptionist: The room's no problem, but you'll have to bath yourself.

Which is which?

Jane found all of these leaves in the park, but she can't remember which tree the leaves came from, or the names of the trees.

Can you help her?

Pair up the leaves with the trees and name them.

Spots before the eyes

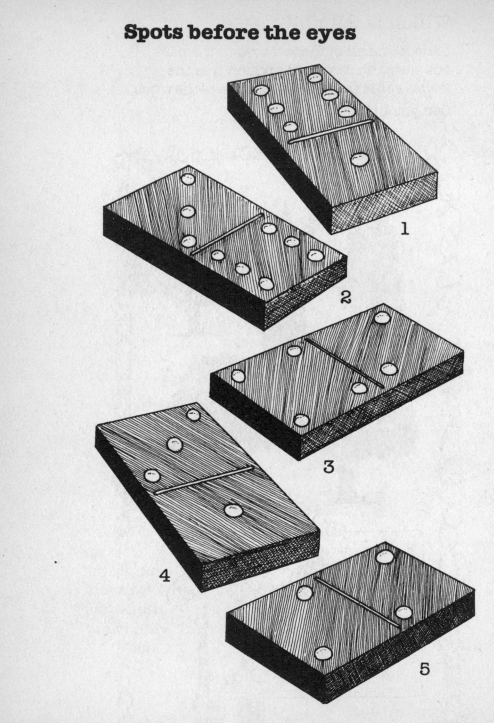

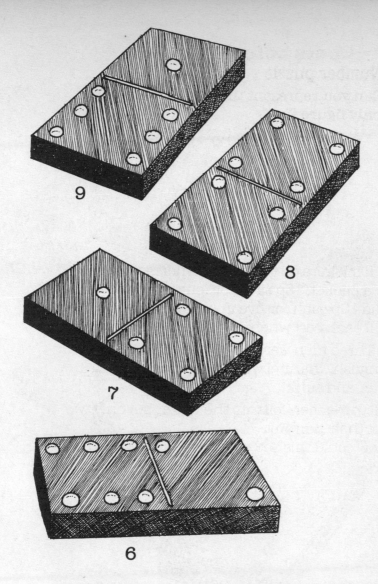

1. Which dominoes have the same total?

2. What is the highest total you can possibly achieve with two dominoes?

3. Draw these dominoes onto a piece of paper. Start with the double two (number 5), and then match the numbers end to end, until they are all used up.

Number puzzle

Can you represent the number 100, using only figure 9's?

Brainteasers

1. If stickers cost 20p each when sold three in a packet, 15p each for four in a packet and 12p each for five in a packet, how much will each cost when sold in a packet of six?

2. Three men were rowing across the English Channel when their boat sprung a leak and sunk.

All three men fell into the water, but only two got their hair wet.
How could this be?

Louise: Sir, would you ever punish me for something I didn't do?
Teacher: No, of course not!
Louise: What a relief! I didn't do my homework.

Which way round?

Can you find your way around this shape in one continuous action?

No line should be traced twice, and once you start you should not break the line!

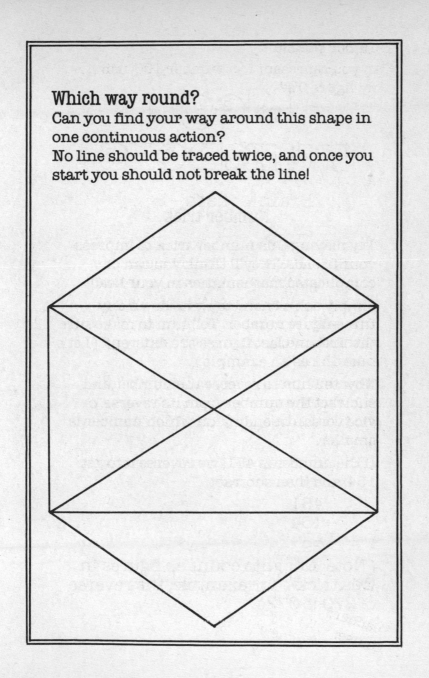

Mega numbers

Number trick

Try playing this number trick to impress your friends. They'll think you can do complicated mathematics in your head!

Simply ask a friend to write down any three-figure number. Tell him to make sure the first and last figures are different. (Let's take 451 as an example).

Now tell him to reverse the number and subtract the number from its reverse, or vice versa, depending on which number is smaller.

If the number is 451, we reverse it to get 154, and then subtract:

$$\begin{array}{r} 451 \\ -154 \\ \hline 297 \end{array}$$

(Note: Noughts count as figures in this trick — for example, the reverse of 270 is 072).

Now tell your friend to reverse the new number and add the new number to its reverse.

$$\begin{array}{r} 297 \\ +792 \\ \hline 1089 \end{array}$$

NOW guess what the final sum is. Whatever number your friend chooses, the answer will always be 1089! You know the secret, but your friends will think you're a genius!

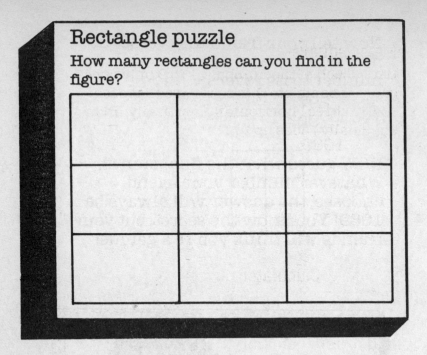

Rectangle puzzle

How many rectangles can you find in the figure?

1st girl   What's green and has two heads and horrible fangs?

2nd girl: I don't know.

1st girl: Neither do I, but it's right behind you!

Q: Why did the chicken cross the road?
A: To get to the other side.

Q: Who can go as fast as a Ferrari?
A: Its driver!

Magic square

Using each of the numbers 1 to 9 only once, can you complete this square so that each row of three (horizontally, vertically, and diagonally) adds up to 15?

8		
		9
		2

Calculator puzzle

Charlotte the computer buff has discovered that she can write the names of the members of her family on her calculator!

She entered the number 318830, turned her calculator upside-down, and found that she had written her mother's name: DEBBIE. Can you figure out the names of the rest of Charlotte's family? Their calculator codes are given below.

Dad: 53719

Uncle: 7718

Auntie: 7717

Cousin: 317537

Brother: 808

Sister: 317719

Here's a code to help you work it out:

9 = G
8 = B
7 = L
5 = S
4 = H
3 = E
1 = I
0 = O or D

Now try to 'write' the names of your own family and friends.

Mind reading

Ask a friend to write down the year
they were born,   1980
Any important year in their life,   1984
How many years have passed
since that year and *this* year
(1993)   9
Ask if they have had a birthday
this year.
If so, ask them to write their age. If
not, ask them to write the age they
will be on their next birthday.   13
                                                           3986

Tell them to add up all the figures
they've written down.

Announce that you will
guess the answer — and
guess 3986! That will be the
answer to this problem for
all of 1993, no matter who
you try it on. For each year
after that, add 2 to the
number you guess (so that
in 1994, the answer will be
3988).

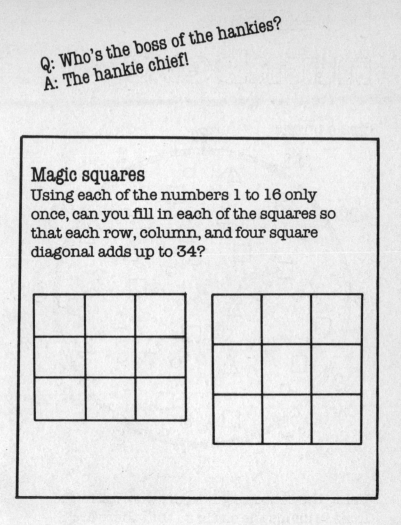

Magic squares
Using each of the numbers 1 to 16 only once, can you fill in each of the squares so that each row, column, and four square diagonal adds up to 34?

Q: What is white and dashes across the desert with a bed pan?
A: Florence of Arabia.

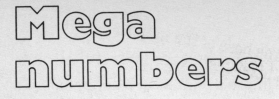

Mega numbers

Circle puzzle

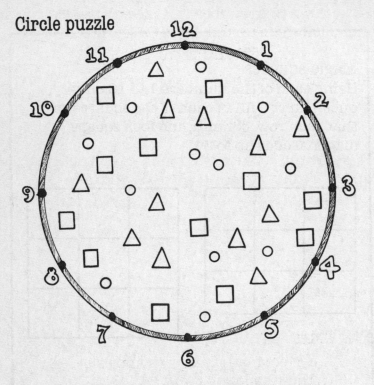

Using the dots as a guide, draw two straight lines to divide the circle so that there are 3 triangles, 3 circles and 3 squares in each section.

1st boy:	I had a toothache and the dentist took my tooth out.
2nd boy:	Does it still hurt?
1st boy:	I don't know – the dentist kept it!

Number trick

Here's a very impressive trick to try on your friends.

Write down this number on a piece of paper and allow them to study it for 30 seconds:

571012151720

Ask them to write it down from memory. Of course, they will fail, but you will be able to write it correctly for them – without even looking at the number again!

The secret to your sudden stroke of genius is that you start with the number 5, and take turns adding 2 and 3 to it:

$5 + 2 = 7$	57
$7 + 3 = 10$	5710
$10 + 2 = 12$	571012
$12 + 3 = 15$	57101215...etc.

Fill it in

Put the correct mathematical symbols ($+$, $-$, or $\times$) in these equations.

5	6	3	=	8
5	3	6	=	9
5	3	6	=	12
5	3	6	=	14
5	3	6	=	90

Puzzle it out

The school cook needs to measure exactly 4 litres of water, but she only has two containers – one holds 3 litres and the other holds 5 litres.

How can she measure exactly 4 litres of water?

1st girl: A bee stung me this morning.
2nd girl: Did you put some cream on it?
1st girl: There wasn't time – it flew away!

Mind reading

Tell a friend to think of a number,		34
double it,	$34 \times 2 =$	68
add 4,	$68 + 4 =$	72
multiply by 5,	$72 \times 5 =$	360
add 12,	$360 + 12 =$	372
and multiply by 10.	$372 \times 10 =$	3720

Ask them for their answer, then subtract
320 from it.

$$
\begin{array}{r}
3720 \\
-\ 320 \\
\hline
3400
\end{array}
$$

Cross of the last two digits of your answer,
and you will be left with your friend's
original number. They'll think you're a
mind-reader!

Knock, knock.
Who's there?
Dwayne.
Dwayne who?
Dwayne the bathtub…I'm dwowning!

Elephant jokes

Q: How do you fit an elephant into a matchbox?

A: Take all the matches out first.

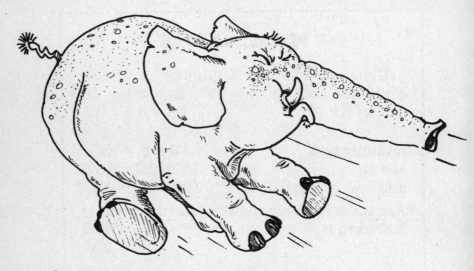

Q: What do you do when an elephant sneezes?

A: Get out of the way!

1st boy: Why do elephants paint their toenails red?

2nd boy: I dunno. Why?

1st boy: So that they can hide in cherry trees without being seen.

2nd boy: That's ridiculous! That would never work!

1st boy: Well, have you ever caught an elephant hiding in a cherry tree?

Q: Where do baby elephants come from?
A: Behind BIG gooseberry bushes!

Q: How do you tell an elephant from a grape?
A: A grape is purple.

Q: How can you tell an elephant from a grape if you are colourblind?
A: Take your shoes off and jump up and down on it. If you don't get any wine, it's an elephant.

Q: What did Jane say?
A: 'Here come the grapes' (She was colourblind).

Q: Why do elephants
wear red tennis
shoes?
A: Because their blue
ones are in the wash.

**Q: Why do elephants
wear green tennis
shoes?**
**A: To sneak across pool
tables without being
seen.**

Q: Why do ducks have
webbed feet?
A: To stamp out forest
fires.

Q: Why do elephants
have flat feet?
A: To stamp out burning
ducks.

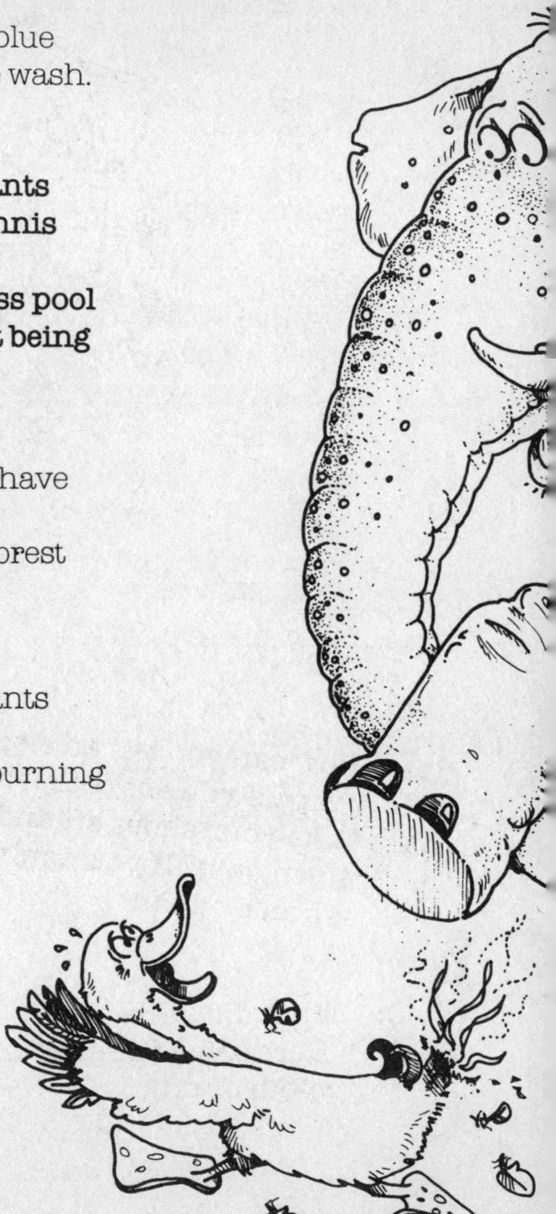

Q: Why do elephants wear sandals?
A: So they don't sink into the sand.

Q: Why do ostriches hide their heads in the sand?
A: To look for elephants who aren't wearing sandals.

Q: Why do elephants float down the river on their backs!
A: To keep their tennis shoes dry.

Look who's appearing in pantomime this Christmas. Can you unravel their names?

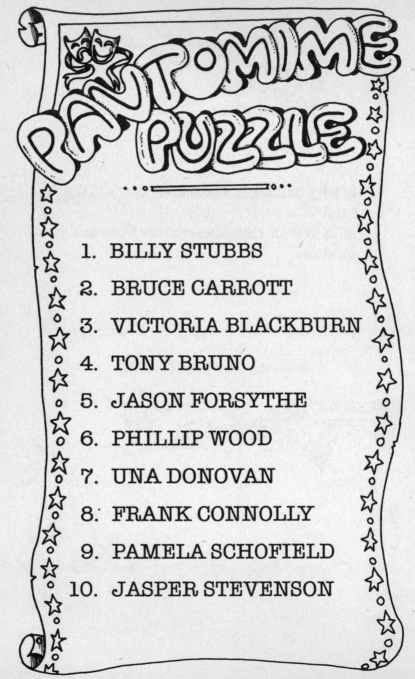

PANTOMIME PUZZLE

1. BILLY STUBBS

2. BRUCE CARROTT

3. VICTORIA BLACKBURN

4. TONY BRUNO

5. JASON FORSYTHE

6. PHILLIP WOOD

7. UNA DONOVAN

8. FRANK CONNOLLY

9. PAMELA SCHOFIELD

10. JASPER STEVENSON

Adult: Kathryn, what will you do when you get as big as me?

Child: Diet!

Mother: Who's that at the door?

Son: A woman with a pram.

Mother: Tell her to push off.

Customer: Is this spray good for flies?

Shop Assistant: Certainly not, sir, it kills them!

Boy: Do you have any cats going cheap?

Pet Salesman: Sorry, son, all of our cats go 'miaow.'

Patient: Doctor, help me! I prefer long socks to short socks!

Psychiatrist: That's not unusual – in fact, so do I!

Patient: What a relief! How do you like yours – baked or fried?

Mega maze

Disc dilemma

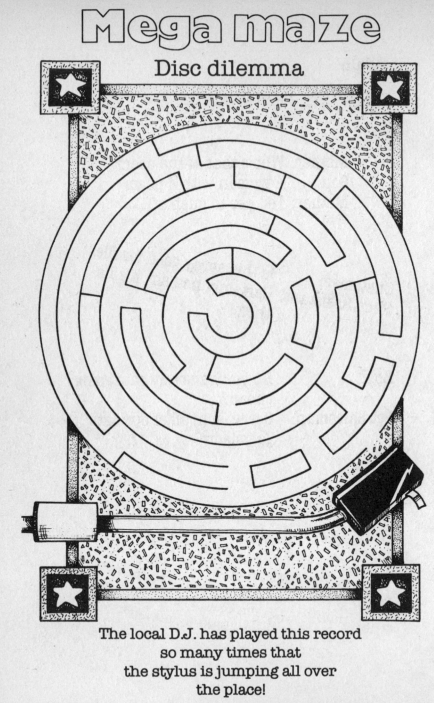

The local D.J. has played this record
so many times that
the stylus is jumping all over
the place!

Follow its precarious path from START to
FINISH!

Mum: I finally got Daniel to stop biting his nails.

Dad: How did you manage that?

Mum: I made him wear shoes!

1st girl: I spend hours staring at my lovely face in the mirror. Do you think I'm vain?

2nd girl: No – insane!

Brainteasers

1. In the O'Grady family there are five brothers and each brother has two sisters. Including the parents, how many are there in the O'Grady family?

2. Is it legal for a man to marry his widow's sister?

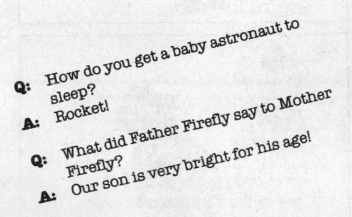

Q: How do you get a baby astronaut to sleep?

A: Rocket!

Q: What did Father Firefly say to Mother Firefly?

A: Our son is very bright for his age!

Head teacher: You said that illness caused you to leave your last school?

Pupil: Yes, the headmaster was sick of me!

Me and my shadow!

These schoolboys look identical in their school uniforms, but are they? Look again and match each boy with his own shadow!

Teacher: Karen! I hope I didn't see you cheating!

Karen: I hope that you didn't, too!

Q: What do you call a gorilla with a submachine gun?

A: 'Sir'!

Odd socks

Gemma is almost dressed for the disco, but a power-cut has plunged her into darkness. She knows, however, that she has 5 bright pink pop-sox and 10 dark blue ones in a drawer. Gemma would like her socks to match, but she doesn't mind if she wears pink or blue. How many must she take out before she can be certain that she has a pair.

Q: What do you call a man with a plank on his head?

A: Edward!

Q: What happened to the man who couldn't tell toothpaste from putty?

A: His windows fell out!

Mystery eggs

Farmer Giles eats two freshly laid eggs every morning. He does not have any hens, neither does he beg, buy or steal the eggs; he doesn't find them or receive them as gifts or even trade for them. Where do the eggs come from?

Knock, knock.
Who's there?
Sarah.
Sarah who?
Sarah doctor in the house.

Q: Why did Robin Hood only steal from the rich?
A: Because the poor had no money!

Upstairs neighbour:	If you don't stop playing those bagpipes, I think I'll lose my mind!
Downstairs neighbour:	Too late — I stopped playing twenty minutes ago!

Q: How many ears did Davy Crockett have?
A: Three: a left ear, a right ear, and a wild frontier.

Boy:	I beat my sister up every morning.
Friend:	Every morning?
Boy:	Yes! I get up at seven and she gets up at eight!

Mega travel

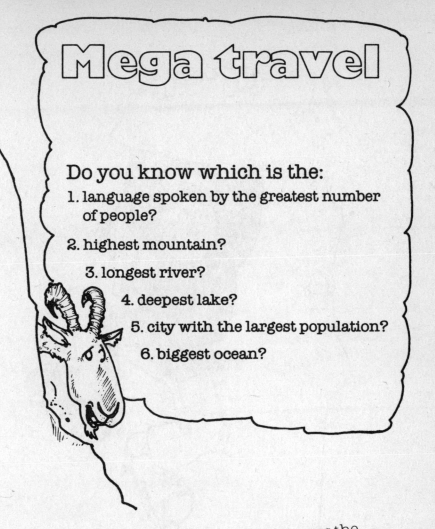

Do you know which is the:

1. language spoken by the greatest number of people?

2. highest mountain?

3. longest river?

4. deepest lake?

5. city with the largest population?

6. biggest ocean?

1st boy: Why did the reporter cross the road?

2nd boy: I don't know.

1st boy: To get the *Peking Tribune*.

2nd boy: I don't get it.

1st boy: Neither do I – I get *The Times*!

Knock, knock.
Who's there?
Otis.
Otis who?
Otis a joy to be alive.

World Trip

Lucky old Larry has won a competition and is going on a trip around the world for his prize.

Unfortunately, there have been some errors on his tickets, and the names of the cities he will be visiting are all jumbled up. Can you unscramble them and discover his route?

Mega travel

Flag puzzle

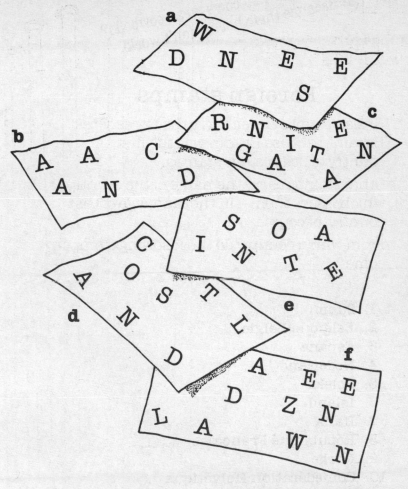

Ernie the caretaker has been asked to hoist the flags for an international competition, but poor old Ernie is confused.

Can you untangle the anagrams above and find out which countries are competing?

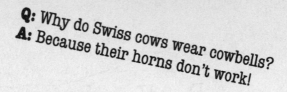
Foreign stamps

British stamps never carry the words 'Great Britain', because Britain was the first country to use postage stamps.

Other stamps carry the name of the country which issues them – in the language of that country, of course.

From which country do the following stamps come?

1. Suomi
2. Belgique/Belgie
3. España
4. Nederland
5. Polska
6. Island
7. Italia
8. République Française
9. Norge
10. Confédération Helvétique

Spot the scenery

Next time you go on a car journey, be it a long one or just around the corner, play this game and make it a fun trip.

Choose something to look for — for example, churches, post boxes, blue cars etc. Before your trip make a 'guestimate' of how many of them you'll see from your car. Each player can write down his guess.

At the end of the journey, see which of your estimates was nearest to the total. Whoever made that guess is the winner!

Q: What can you see in winter that is invisible in summer?
A: Your breath!

Knock, knock.
Who's there?
Winnie.
Winnie who?
Winnie you going to let me in?

Jerry: Mum, all the kids call me 'teacher's pet'!
Mum: Why is that, dear?
Jerry: Because she keeps me in a cage!

Etiquette is learning to yawn with your mouth closed.

Q: Why is Lord Litchfield like a novel?
A: They both have titles!

Q: Does your digital watch tell the time?
A: No, I have to look at it!

Silly verse
I had written to Aunt Maud
Who was on a trip abroad,
When I heard she'd died of cramp
Just too late to save the stamp.

Time shattering!

Grandma Jess's mantelpiece clock crashed
onto the floor, and its face
broke in half. The numbers
on one side added up to 35,
and on the other side
they added up to 43.
How did the clock's face break?

New Employee: How many people work here?

Foreman: Oh, about one out of every ten!

Brainteaser

What is the next letter in this sequence:

O T T F F S S

Q: What game do elephants play in cars?

A: Squash!

Q: Why was Cinderella bad at tennis?

A: Because her coach was a pumpkin!

Q: What's the difference between a buffalo and a bison?

A: You can't wash your hands in a buffalo!

Boy: My cat sleeps with me at night.

Girl: Yuck! That's unhealthy!

Boy: I know, but he doesn't mind.

Maze

Ben's mother is talking to him, but what she is saying is just going in one ear and out of the other!

Start from IN and, following the direction of the arrows, trace the lines until you come to OUT at the other side.

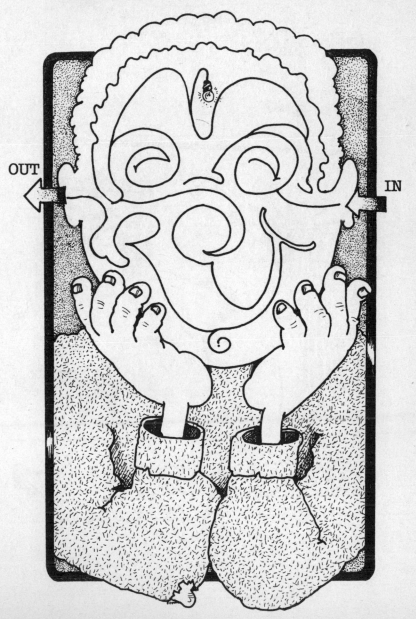

OUT

IN

Mother: Son, *must* you scratch yourself?
Son: Yes, Mother – no one else knows where I itch!

Mother: Don't bring that dog in the house, Jim – it's full of fleas!
Jim: Did you hear that, Fido? Don't go in the house – Mum says it's full of fleas!

Brainteasers

1. Standing on the pavement, how can you drop an egg 1 metre without breaking it?

2. Can you think of a five letter word which has only one consonant?

Q: How do get four elephants in a Mini?
A: Two in the back and two in the front!

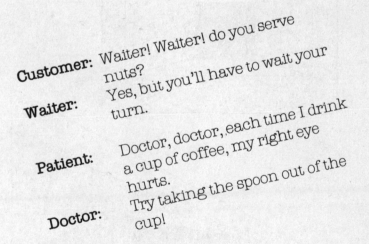

Customer: Waiter! Waiter! do you serve nuts?
Waiter: Yes, but you'll have to wait your turn.

Patient: Doctor, doctor, each time I drink a cup of coffee, my right eye hurts.
Doctor: Try taking the spoon out of the cup!

Colour it in

Did you know that you never need more than four colours to fill in every section of a map or design so that no two adjoining sections share the same colours? (Some designs can, of course, be coloured using less than four).

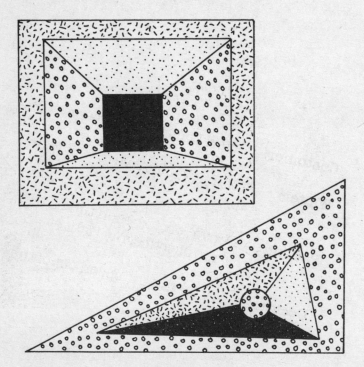

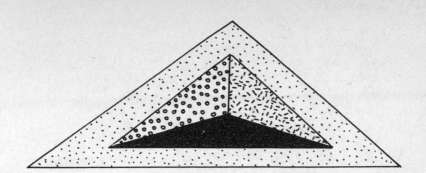

Examples:

Even the most intricate patterns (like the one below) do not need more than four colours. This fact can be proved using very complicated mathematics. No one has yet found one that needs five colours — not even a computer!

Now try some patterns of your own. You might just prove the mathematics wrong!

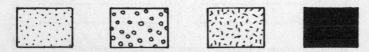

Army puzzle

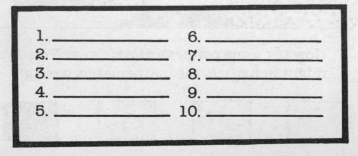

Sergeant
General
Private
Colonel
Corporal
Captain
Warrant Officer
Major
Brigadier
Lieutenant

Corporal David Smith hopes to become a general one day, but he has a long way to go!

Can you put these army ranks in rising order to find out just how far he has yet to go?

1. _____   6. _____
2. _____   7. _____
3. _____   8. _____
4. _____   9. _____
5. _____   10. _____

Knock, knock.
Who's there?
Scott.
Scott who?
Scott nothing to do with you.

Knock, knock.
Who's there?
Scold.
Scold who?
Scold outside! Let me in!

Knock, knock.
Who's there?
Harriet.
Harriet who?
Harriet three ice creams and now he feels
sick.

Knock, knock.
Who's there?
Carmen.
Carmen who?
Carmen over to my house.

Knock, knock.
Who's there?
Hyde.
Hyde who?
Hyde like to tell you but it's a secret.

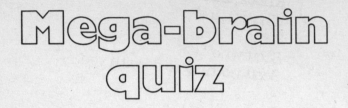

Mega-brain quiz

1. What is the name of the largest desert in Africa?
2. Who is Popeye's girlfriend?
3. Who was the first man in space?
4. Which Greek king made everything he touched turn to gold?
5. Why are ladybirds good for the garden?
6. Who was the first president of the U.S.A.?
7. Where did the first modern Olympic games take place?
8. How many miles are run in a marathon?
9. What was the former name of Iran?
10. Is Beaujolais a red, or a white wine?
11. What is an Aberdeen Angus?
12. Why is helium gas used to fill balloons?
13. Which planet is called 'the red planet'?
14. What is an Eskimo's home called?
15. Which disciple betrayed Jesus?
16. What are the two types of elephant?
17. Who was 'the king of rock and roll'?

18. Which country has a maple leaf as its national emblem?

19. Name all four Beatles.

20. What is the former name of Thailand?

21. On which continent is most of the world's coffee grown?

22. When it's twelve noon in London, what time is it in New York?

23. What is a 'troglodyte'?

24. Which artist spent three years on his back, painting the ceiling of the Sistine Chapel in the Vatican?

25. Which substance has the molecular name H_2O?

Mega sports

Crossword

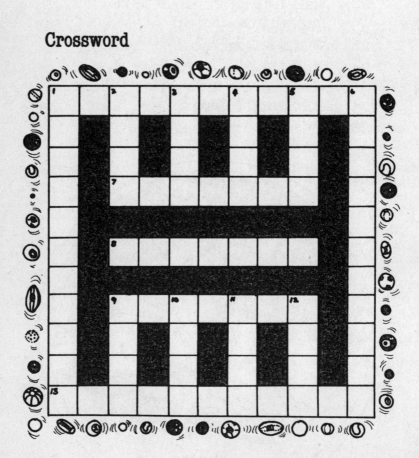

Across:

1. The most famous cricket matches. (4, 7)
7. Cricket teams! (7)
8. It's similar to basketball. (7)
9. Could be referees. (7)
13. You can get a lift from these. (11)

Down:

1. There's a famous centre one. (6, 5)
2. Which _ _ _ _ are you on?
3. Coe, Ovett and Cram have run this distance well. (4)
4. Half-_ _ _ _ (4)
5. Before steps and jumps. (4)
6. They play 'in place of.' (11)
9. A European Cup organisation. (4 initials)
10. He holds up the scrum. (4)
11. Not the imaginary part of Madrid. (4)
12. Used to make bowling quite tricky. (4)

Coach: Why didn't you stop that ball?
Goalie: That's what the net's for, isn't it?

Mega sports

An Englishman, a Frenchman, and an American stood on the rostrum to receive medals for winning the Olympic long jump event. But can you guess who won the gold medal, who the silver, and who the bronze?

The shortest athlete beat the tallest one, and the one whose flag has stars on it came in second. In which order did they place?

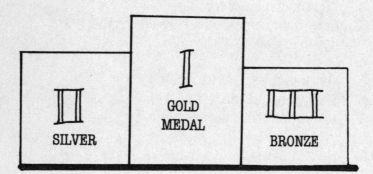

Rick: Who are the fans booing at?
Roger: That man who threw a rock at the referee.
Rick: But it missed, didn't it?
Roger: That's why they're booing!

Q: If umpires are in cricket, and referees are in football, what are in bowls?

A: Goldfish!

Q: Why did Cinderella get thrown out of the rounders team?

A: Because she kept running away from the ball!

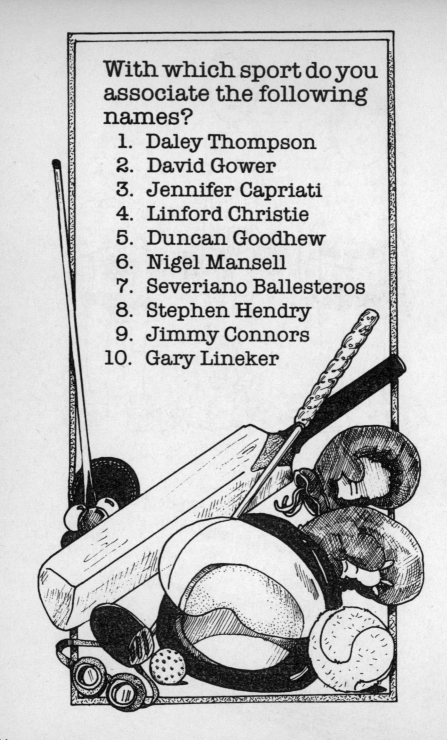

With which sport do you associate the following names?

1. Daley Thompson
2. David Gower
3. Jennifer Capriati
4. Linford Christie
5. Duncan Goodhew
6. Nigel Mansell
7. Severiano Ballesteros
8. Stephen Hendry
9. Jimmy Connors
10. Gary Lineker

Mother: Why were you late for breakfast?

Son: I had a dream about a football match.

Mother: Why does that make you late for breakfast?

Son: Well, they played extra time.

Football muddle

Our sports reporter has got his notes a bit muddled up. Can you unravel these football club names for him?

1. West Hotspur
2. Crystal Wednesday
3. Nottingham Argyle
4. Aston United
5. Plymouth Rovers
6. Sheffield Ham
7. Manchester Villa
8. Leyton Palace
9. Tottenham Forest
10. Bristol Orient

Olympigram

Even fat old Frank is a keen Olympic Games fan. He can remember all kinds of athletes, incidents and records. But he can't remember which cities have hosted the Games. Can you unscramble the names of some of the Olympic host cities which are jumbled up above

He: This is not my shirt! The collar is so tight I can barely breathe!

She: Don't be silly. You've got your head through the buttonhole.

Brainteaser

One day Rod and John went off to play in the paddock adjoining their new friend's home. They were very surprised to find a carrot and two pieces of coal in the middle of the paddock. Their friend's house has no coal fires nor a vegetable patch. Can you think of how the carrot and coal got there?

1st Boy: Do you know the joke about the broken pencil?

2nd Boy: No.

1st Boy: Well, there's no point to it, anyway!

Picture puzzle

James is keen on art. He has copied this picture from his bedroom wall. He thought it was a perfect copy, but there are in fact five errors. Can you spot them?

MATCHSTICK PUZZLES

Use some used matches or toothpicks to solve these puzzles:

Puzzle 1

Make this pattern, and remove 6 matches to leave 10.

Puzzle 2

Can you arrange 12 matches to form 5 squares?

Can you arrange 24 matches to form 14 squares?

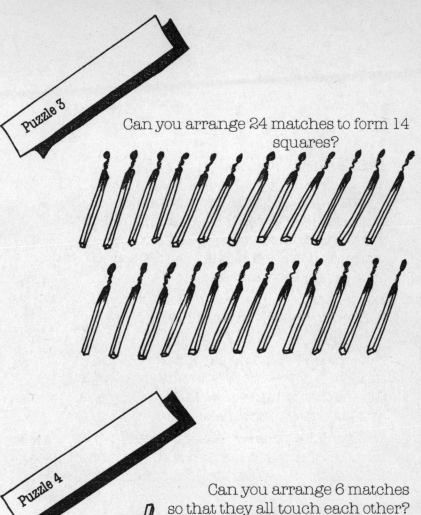

Can you arrange 6 matches so that they all touch each other?

Mega dots

This is a game of skill for two. Your goal is to finish more squares than your opponent. If you put the fourth side on a square, it's yours! And every time you complete a square, you have another turn.

All you need is a pencil. At each turn, you connect two dots, either horizontally or vertically.

But beware of putting the third side on a square! Then your opponent might complete the square for himself, write his initial in it, and get a free turn as well!

When all the lines are drawn, count up the number of squares marked with your initial. If you have more than your opponent does, you win.

If you lost, make a new grid on blank paper, and get your revenge!

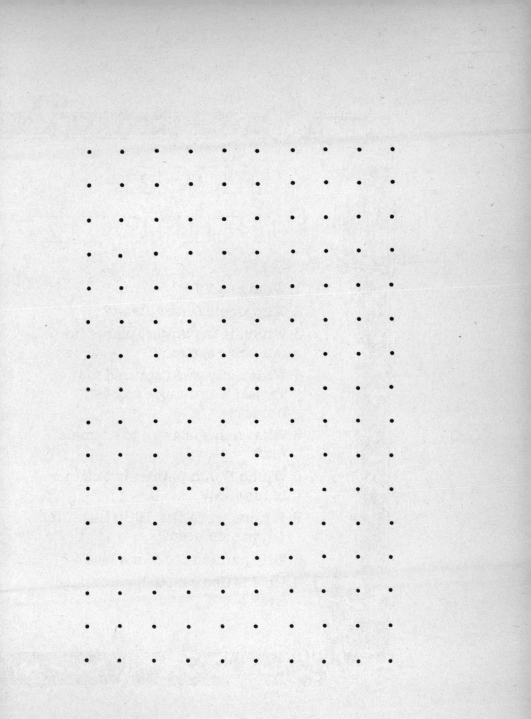

223

Mega-brain quiz

1. What is a V.I.P?

2. Who wrote *Oliver Twist*?

3. Which is the largest planet in our solar system?

4. Which city was captured in the Trojan War using a wooden horse?

5. What name is given to a female fox?

6. Which Dutch painter cut off one of his ears?

7. Where were the 1988 Summer Olympics held?

8. Who painted the Mona Lisa?

9. How is God said to have created Eve?

10. Which Italian city was destroyed when Mount Vesuvius erupted?

11. In which city does the pope live?

12. What did the Queen of Hearts bake?

13. What did Jason and the Argonauts seek?

14. What is the official language of Israel?

15. What is a Red Admiral?

Mega words

Watch your spelling

The objects in each of the pairs below have names that sound alike, but are spelt differently. (Such pairs of words are called homophones). Can you label each object correctly?

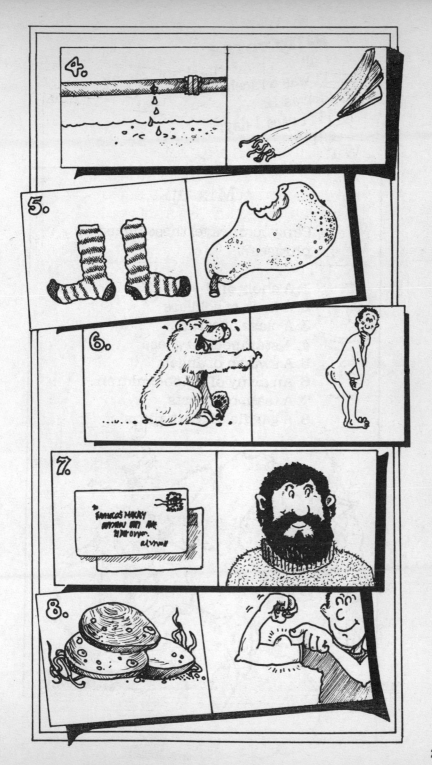

227

Silly verse

Can you read this simple rhyme?

11 was a racehorse;
22 was 12.
1111 race 1 day;
22112!

Mix-up

Can you unravel these mixed-up phrases?

1. A choir of sheep
2. A flock of soldiers
3. A class of cattle
4. A stampede of geese
5. A swarm of angels
6. An army of schoolchildren
7. A team of insects
8. A gaggle of footballers

Mega words

Word study

The following words mean the study of a certain subject:

**philately   astrology
astronomy   radiology
graphology**

Can you put the correct title under the pictorial clues below?

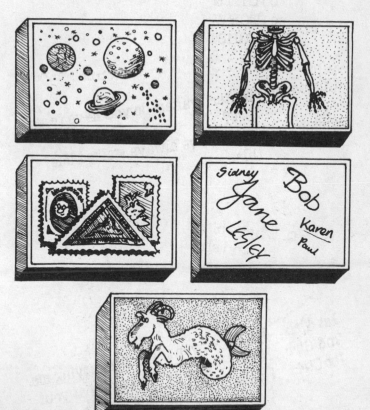

Customer: Waiter, waiter! My egg is bad!
Waiter: That's not my fault, sir. I only laid the table.

Do you know?

1. Which English word contains all 5 vowels in the correct order? (AEIOU)
2. Which words contain the following combinations of consonants?
   a) CKST
   b) GHTN
   c) TCHW
   d) TCHST

Customer: Waiter! waiter! do you have frogs' legs?
Waiter: No, sir, I've always walked like this.

Q: What's black, and shoots out of the ground shouting, 'Knickers!'
A: Crude oil.

1st Girl: That boy over there is annoying me.
2nd Girl: Him? He's not even looking at you!
1st Girl: I know...that's what's so annoying.

Palindrome puzzle

Can you find five palindromes for these clues? (A palindrome is a word or sentence that reads the same way backwards as forwards – for example, 'deed' or 'level').

a) They used to rule Iran.
b) To cover the sitting room wall again
c) Musical compositions for one instrument
d) Tales from Scandinavia
e) She lives in a convent.

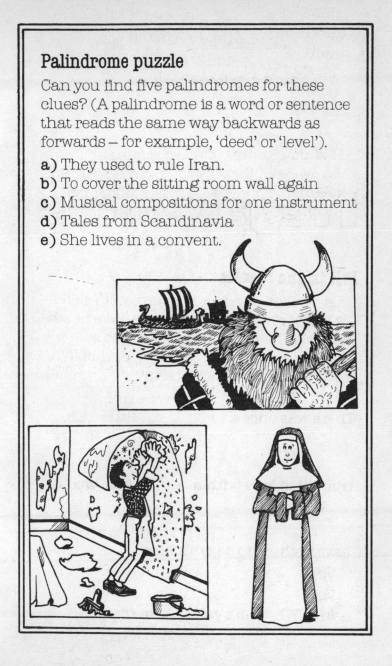

Photo fun

Old Mr Mullens has found a family photo! As he admires it he proudly exclaims:
'Brothers and sisters have I none,
But that man's father is my father's son.'
Who is in the picture?

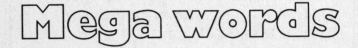

Fill in the blanks

Help a friend create a masterpiece! You call out the parts of speech written underneath these blanks, and fill in your friend's answers. Then, when the story is complete, read them the hilarious result!

There was once a _____ **little** ____
adjective   noun

who fell in love with a _____ **who would**
noun

have nothing to do with him. _____ **, he**
adverb

asked, 'Why don't you ____ **me?'**
verb

'Your _____ are too _____ ,' was
    plural noun   adjective

the reply. He became very _____ . What
                          adjective

could be done? He _____ his
                   verb (past tense)

_____ , and _____ asked, 'How can I ____
noun   adverb   verb

the _____ ?'
   noun

' _____ !' was the response.
  exclamation

'A _____ of _____ ing will fix that!'
    period of time   verb

_____ , the little fellow _____
adverb   verb (past tense)

this_____ advice. And soon, his _____
    adjective   nouns

were as _____ as could be expected.
        adjective

' _____ !' he cried. 'The ____ is on!'
  exclamation   noun

Shopping list

There are only six items on the shopping list, but it looks as if there are many more! Can you find out what they are by solving these clues?

Start by naming the pictured objects — then subtract letters from the name, as instructed.

Example:

Optical illusion

What's wrong with this table? How many legs has it got?

If you said six, cover the bottom part of the legs with your hand, and guess again! See if you can figure out the trick that makes this illusion work.

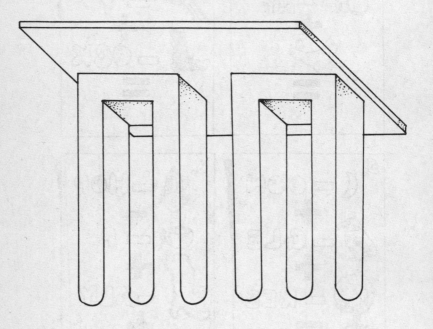

Athlete: I think I'm hurt. Better call me a doctor.

Coach: All right – you're a doctor!

Lou: Dad, I can't eat this hamburger. It's awful!

Dad: Shall I call the waiter?

Lou: No, I don't think even he'll be able to eat it.

Thin writing

Can you read these three words? If not, hold the page level with your nose and try again. It might help to close one eye as well.

Now try writing your own thin writing. Can your friends read their own thin names?

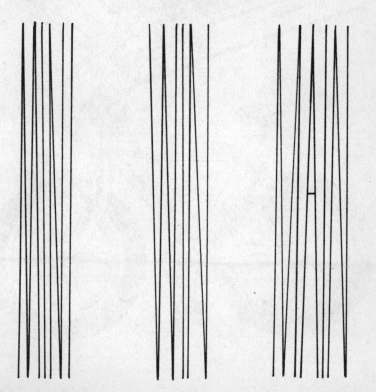

Test yourself

Study this page for just 30 seconds. Then cover the book and see how many objects you can remember in the next 30 seconds.

Test your friends and family. Who do you find has the better memory – the adults or the children?

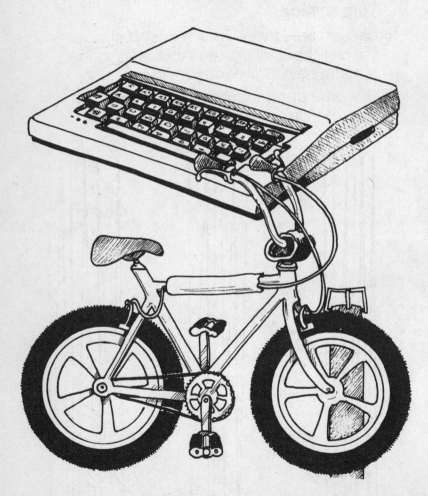

Mega morse

Study this Morse Code alphabet to work out the messages **opposite**:

A	.-		N	-.
B	-...		O	---
C	-.-.		P	.--.
D	-..		Q	--.-
E	.		R	.-.
F	..-.		S	...
G	--.		T	-
H	....		U	..-
I	..		V	...-
J	.---		W	.--
K	-.-		X	-..-
L	.-..		Y	-.--
M	--		Z	--..

Q: What's red and spotty and cries all the time?

A: A love-sick ladybird!

Mother: Would you like to join me in a bowl of soup?

G'mother: Do you think there will be enough room for us both.

Can you write your name in Morse Code? Try writing the names of the members of your family, too.

Navy lark

Charles Samuels is a naval Commander. Do you know which of the ranks listed below are senior to him and which are junior to him?

Arrange them in order, starting with the lowest rank, and write them in the spaces below.

One of them is done for you.

Fleet Chief Petty Officer	1.
Lieutenant	2. Fleet Chief Petty Officer
Captain	3.
Commander	4.
Admiral	5.
Midshipman	6.
Able Seaman	7.
Lieutenant Commander	8.
Sub Lieutenant	9.

Puzzle picture

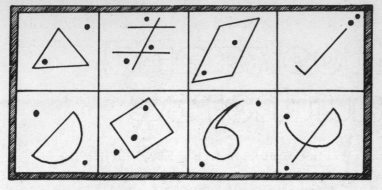

Which two pictures are the odd men out?

Baby Margaret never made a sound – not a cry or a coo. For seven years she didn't speak, and her parents gave up hope of ever hearing her voice.

Then one night at dinner, she took a bite of her potatoes, made a face, and said, 'Needs salt.'

'Oh, my!' said her mother. 'Why have you never spoken before?'

'Well,' replied Margaret, 'up until now, everything's been okay.'

Mack: You must think I'm a perfect idiot.

Mabel: No, I don't...nobody's perfect!

Books and authors

Can you use names from the list to fill in who wrote the books:
(Some letters have been filled in to help you).

a) ROBERT LOUIS STEVENSON
b) LEWIS CARROLL
c) CHARLES DICKENS
d) KENNETH GRAHAME
e) GEORGE ORWELL
f) JOHN WYNDHAM

MEGA BRAIN QUIZ

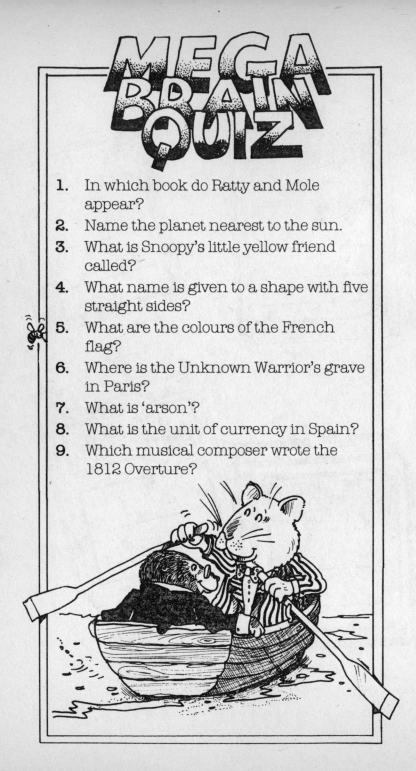

1. In which book do Ratty and Mole appear?
2. Name the planet nearest to the sun.
3. What is Snoopy's little yellow friend called?
4. What name is given to a shape with five straight sides?
5. What are the colours of the French flag?
6. Where is the Unknown Warrior's grave in Paris?
7. What is 'arson'?
8. What is the unit of currency in Spain?
9. Which musical composer wrote the 1812 Overture?

10. Where was William Shakespeare born?
11. What is the normal temperature of the human body?
12. What is Braille?
13. On which river does Rome stand?
14. Who invented the telephone?
15. One of the most beautiful buildings in the world is at Agra in India. What is its name?
16. What is the capital of France?
17. What game do you play with a shuttlecock?
18. What is the sixth colour in the rainbow?

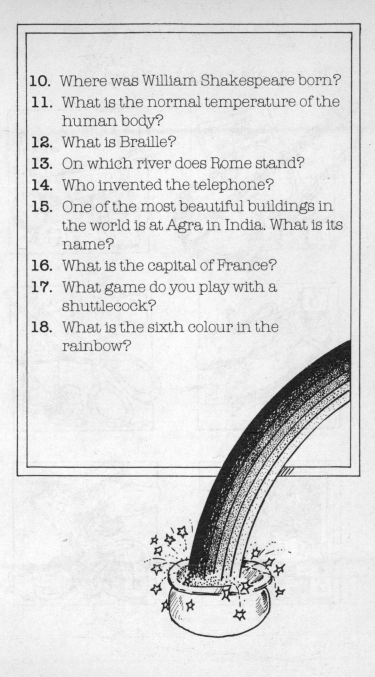

Occupational hazard

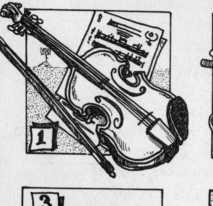

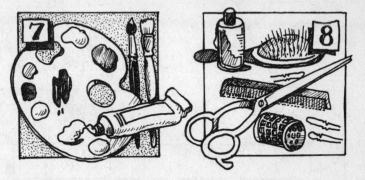

Pictured above are the tools of various trades. See if you can match the objects with their owners' words below!

a) 'Plié, pirouette, et arabesque!'
b) 'Do you want this next bit *forte* or *mezzoforte*?'
c) 'A little off the top?'
d) 'Jones, please answer. What is the capital of France?'
e) 'I'm striving for an impressionistic style.'
f) 'The problem with perennials is that they need a lot of work.'
g) 'Including the selvages in straight-edge facings saves clean-finishing them.'
h) 'Without my anvil, I'd be nowhere.'

Try this animal cross-word puzzle!

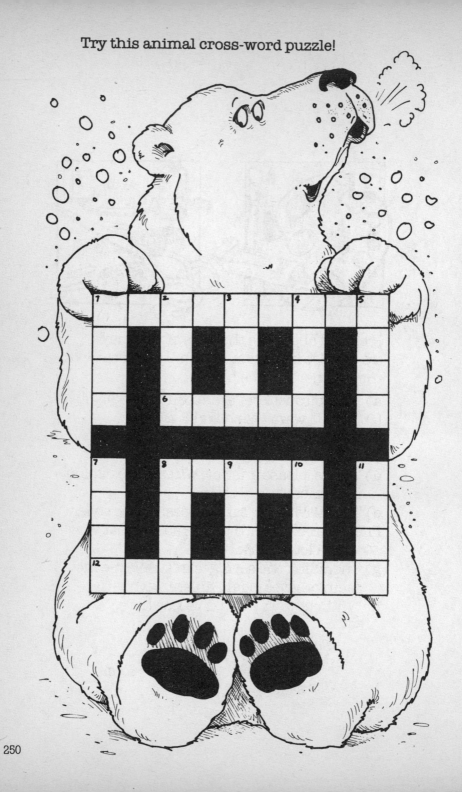

Across:

1. Big white teddy! (5, 4)
6. Healthy dogs have cold _ _ _ _ _. (5)
8. A kind of pet fish. (7)
12. Spotted dog. (9)

Down:

1. _ _ _ _ -in-Boots. (4)
2. King of beasts. (4)
3. The Pied Piper's followers. (4)
4. Fishy snakes! (4)
5. This black bird should be good at chess! (4)
7. Reptiles are _ _ _ _ -blooded animals. (4)
8. Common sea bird. (4)
9. Mountain lion. (4)
10. Abominable snow-man. (4)
11. A graceful water bird. (4)

Q: When is it bad luck to see a black cat?
A: When you're a white mouse

Knock, knock.
Who's there?
Egbert.
Egbert who?
Egbert no bacon.

Patient: Doctor, doctor, I keep thinking I'm invisible.
Doctor: Who said that?

Several dangerous animals are lurking in this picture. Can you unscramble the words to find out what they are?

LUVREUT

KONMEY

PHELANTE

NOLI

ANSEKS

HOPIP

DICCOROLE

RETGI

Q: What kind of nuts sneeze the most?
A: Cashews !

Q: Why do birds fly south for the winter?
A: Because it's too far to walk!

Q: What is yellow and always points North?
A: A magnetized banana!

Q: How do you take a lion's temperature?
A: Very carefully!

Q: Why does a traffic warden have a yellow band around her hat?
A: So that you don't park on her head!

Customer: Waiter, waiter! My egg is bad!
Waiter: That's not my fault, sir. I only laid the table.

Customer: Waiter, waiter! Will you bring me a coffee without cream?
Waiter: Sorry, sir, we're out of cream. Will you have it without milk?

Customer: Waiter, waiter! There's a fly in my soup!
Waiter: Don't worry, Sir: that spider on your toast will get it!

A policeman saw an old man dragging a box on a lead, and thought he'd better humour him. He stepped up to the old man and said,

'That's a nice dog you've got there.'

'It's not a dog – it's a box,' replied the man.

'Oh, excuse me,' laughed the policeman, and he walked on.

The man turned to the box and said, 'Fooled him that time, didn't we, Fido?'

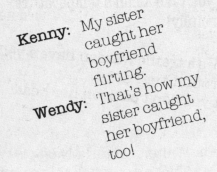

Kenny: My sister caught her boyfriend flirting.

Wendy: That's how my sister caught her boyfriend, too!

Q: How does a skeleton eat his supper?
A: From bone china!

Q: Which trees have no bark and no leaves?
A: Shoe trees!

Boyfriend: Mr. Smith, I've come to ask for your daughter's hand in marriage.

Father: Sorry, son…you've got to take all of her, or nothing!

Silly verse

Willy, with a thirst for gore,
Nailed his sister to the door.
Mother said, with humour quaint,
'Now, Willie dear, don't scratch the paint.'

1st Boy: That girl over there just rolled her eyes at me.

2nd Boy: Well, pick them up and roll them back to her.

Q: What did Tarzan say when he saw a stampeding herd of elephants?

A: 'Here come the elephants!'

Q: What did Tarzan say when he saw the elephants wearing dark glasses?

A: Nothing! He didn't recognize them!

Q: What does it mean when you see five elephants approaching you in identical blue and black sweatshirts?

A: They're all on the same team.

Rings before the eyes

Guess how many circles there are in this pattern. Then count them and find out if you are close!

Rover has fallen down to the bottom of a fifteen metre well. Each day he clambers up three metres and slips back two. How many days will it take him to get out?

257

Can you remember?

Study these pictures. Now close the book! Can you make a list of all the objects you have seen? There are 20 in all.

Mega illusion
Which line is longer: A or B?

Patient: Doctor, are you sure I'm okay? I heard of a man who was treated for a cold, and he died of malaria!

Doctor: Don't worry, my man: when *I* treat a patient for a cold, he *dies* of a cold.

Miss Franklin: Billy, can you prove that the world is round?

Billy: I never said it was.

Trainer: What makes you think that you'll make a good runner?

Boy: Well, I've already got athlete's foot!

Silly verse

Peas

I eat my peas with honey,
I've done it all my life.
It makes the peas taste funny,
But it keeps them on the knife.

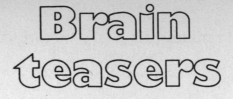
Brain teasers

1. In the Kent orchards the world's finest pear tree grows. It has a trunk three metres in diameter, and exactly 15 branches. Each branch splits into 6 twigs and every twig bears 1 fruit. How many plums on the tree?

2. Big John and his two small mates are on the run from the police. To escape they must cross the River Thames. Big John weighs 100 kilos and his mates each weigh 50 kilos. They find a rowing boat but it can only carry 100 kilos. How can they cross?

Q: **What does Dracula take at night?**
A: **A coffin break.**

Q: Where do Vikings drink?
A: At a Norse trough.

Q: What kind of fish has two knees?
A: A tu-nee fish!

Anna: I have the face of a 19-year-old.

Fred: Well, you'd better give it back — you're getting it all wrinkled.

Triangle tease

How many triangles can you find in the figure?

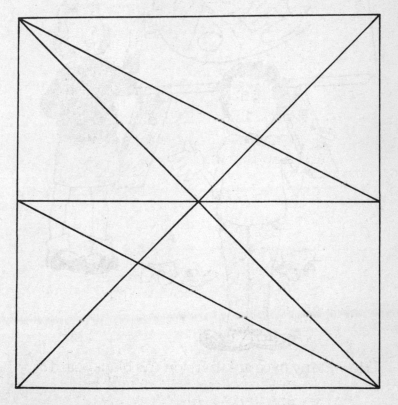

Figure it out

How many fives are there on the blackboard?

Q: How do you make a Maltese Cross?
A: Stamp on his foot.

Robert: I can jump higher than a double decker bus!
Nicholas: I'll bet you £5 you can't.
Robert: You owe me £5. A double decker bus can't jump at all!

Q: Why is there a policeman sitting in that tree?
A: He thinks he's been transferred to a special branch!

1st boy: How did you do with the exam questions?
2nd boy: I did well with the questions, but I had trouble with the answers!

Magistrate: This is not the first time that you have been up before me, is it?
Prisoner: I don't know, sir. I usually get up at 8.00 am. What about you?

Picture puzzle

Unscramble these labels and pair the objects that rhyme.

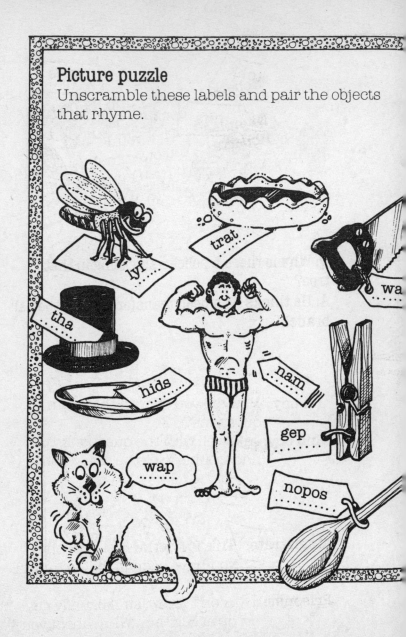

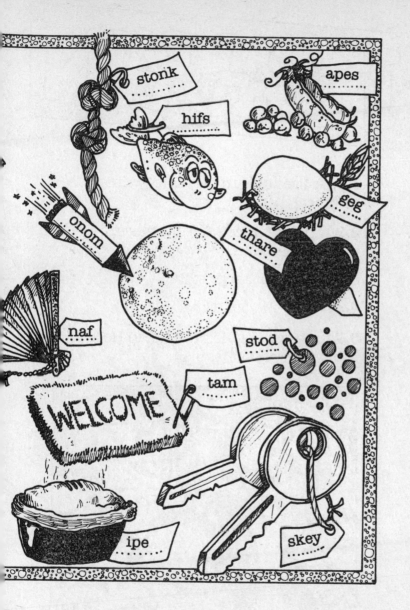

stonk
....

apes
....

hifs
....

geg
....

onom
....

thare
....

naf
....

stod
....

tam
....

WELCOME

ipe
....

skey
....

267

MEGA-BRAIN

1. Who lives in Number 10, Downing Street?

2. Who wrote *Alice's Adventures in Wonderland*?

3. What is a 'poltergeist'?

4. What is the capital of Poland?

5. Where was the home of Robin Hood and his Merry Men?

6. Who is the patron saint of travel?

7. Which of the seven wonders of the ancient world is standing today?

8. What is caviar?

9. What is Elton John's real name?

10. Who was the Roman god of war?

11. What is the currency of Italy?

12. Where is Red Square?

13. What special name is given to the boats used in Venice?

14. What was the name of the first artificial satellite?

15. Of what nationality was the painter Picasso?

16. What is the longest mountain range in the world?

17. What is the name of the tiger in *The Jungle Book*?

18. Which sport made Bjorn Borg famous?

Q: What's the best thing to do if a bull charges you?
A: Pay him!

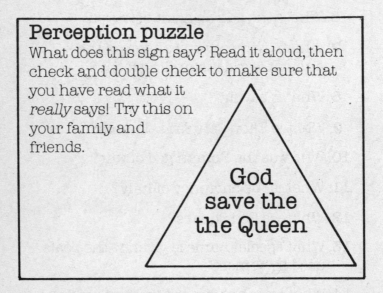

Perception puzzle

What does this sign say? Read it aloud, then check and double check to make sure that you have read what it *really* says! Try this on your family and friends.

God
save the
the Queen

1st Man: Have you seen a policeman around here?
2nd Man: No.
1st Man: Can you tell me where the nearest police station is?
2nd Man: No.
1st Man: Right, then: stick 'em up!

Spot the film

There's a star-studded film festival opening soon! Unfortunately, the posters have been badly printed. What are the films?

Mega-pop

Do you know who's who (or what) in the pop world? Try this pop crossword puzzle and find out!

Across:

1. Cult band from the sixties
5. ------ Quo
6. Shiny Happy People
7. The answer is Simple -----
8. The King
10. Second name of this band: young plant!

Down:

2. They are crazy!
3. John, Paul, George and Ringo – collectively!
4. See 9 down
7. Christian name of lead singer of the band that gathers no moss!
9. ---- N' ----- (with 4 down)

Secretary: The Invisible Man is here to see you, sir.

Boss: Tell him I can't possibly see him!

TOP TEN TEASER

Here are ten top bands and recording artistes who have often been in the Top Ten. Unravel their names to find out who they are.

1. ELVIS MICHAEL

2. ROLLING MINOGUE

3. BEE RED

4. KYLIE COLLINS

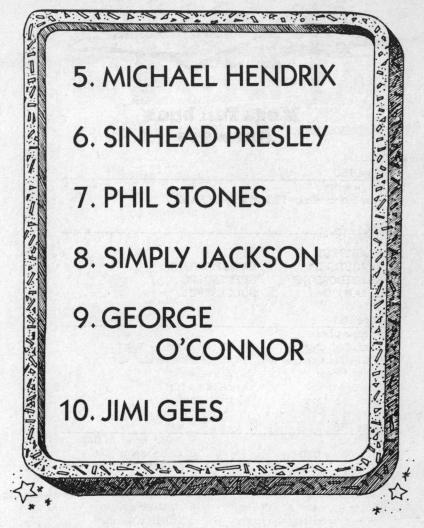

5. MICHAEL HENDRIX

6. SINHEAD PRESLEY

7. PHIL STONES

8. SIMPLY JACKSON

9. GEORGE O'CONNOR

10. JIMI GEES

Mega fun book
Answers

Page 150
Mega words
A coded message I LIKE ICE CREAM!

Page 152
Fill it in
BEAUTIFUL
FAVOURITE   SATISFACTORY
KALEIDOSCOPE   SPECTACLES
GIGANTIC   SUCCESSFUL

Page 153
Phrase phase
Purr of an engine.   Neigh of a horse.
Blast of an explosion.   Gobble of a Turkey.
Roar of a lion.   Hoot of an owl.
Tick of a clock.   Crack of a whip.
Slam of a door.   Whistle of a kettle.

Page 156
Fill it in
1. A queer **fish**
2. Have a **bee** in one's bonnet
3. It's raining **cats** and **dogs**
4. Smell a **rat**
5. Let the **cat** out of the bag
6. Take a **bull** by the horns
7. Act the **goat**
8. **Horse** play
9. A fine kettle of **fish**
10. As the **crow** flies
11. A **cat** on hot bricks
12. A **bird's** eye view
13. Dead as a **dodo**
14. No **flies** on him
15. The **lion's** share
16. A **fly** in the ointment
17. A **dog** in the manger
18. Stubborn as a **mule**

Page 157
Brainteaser
There's no such thing as half a hole!

Page 158
Captivating question
The question is: 'Which door will the other guard tell me is the door to Robin's cell?'

(The lying guard knows that the truthful guard would tell Marion the correct door, so he will lie and say the wrong one. The truthful guard knows that the liar would lie, so he will also say the wrong door.)

Page 160
Classroom chaos
Nun, noon, did, dud, deed, peep, pip, eye, pop, pup, ewe, pep, poop. Did you find any others?

Page 161
True or False?
1. False. They both have the same number.
2. False. The capital of the United States is Washington, D.C.
3. True.
4. False. A Palomino is a golden coloured horse with a white mane and tail.
5. False. Bleriot was the first man to fly across the English Channel.
6. True. Shirley Crabtree is Big Daddy's real name.
7. False. The top score is 180 (3 times triple 20).
8. False. Oregano is the herb; origami is a form of Japanese paper sculpture.
9. False. Ben Nevis is Britain's highest mountain.
10. True.

Page 162
Odd one out
1. CABBAGE – The others grow underground.
2. ZEBRA – The others are carnivores (meat eaters).
3. PIGEON – The others are swimming birds.
4. PINEAPPLE – The others grow on trees.
5. MANCHESTER – The others are capital cities.
6. NYLON – The others are natural fibres and are not man-made.

Page 163
Which is which?
1. Pine tree – its leaf is b.
2. Poplar tree – its leaf is c.
3. Horse chestnut tree – its leaf is d.
4. Oak tree – its leaf is a.
5. Weeping willow – its leaf is e.

Page 164
Spots before the eyes
1. Numbers 1 and 9; numbers 6 and 8; numbers 4 and 5.
2. Number 2 joins number 8 and equals 17.
3. Here is one way of doing it. Have you found any others?

Page 166
Number puzzle
99%
Brainteesers
1. 10p. Every packet costs 60p, regardless of how many it contains.
2. One of the men was bald.

Page 167
Which way round?

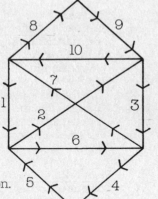

Page 170
Rectangle puzzle
35

Page 171
Magic square

There is only one possible configuration.

8	3	4
1	5	9
6	7	2

Calculator puzzle
Dad: GILES   Auntie: LILL   Brother: BOB
Uncle: BILL   Cousin: LESLIE   Sister: GILLIE

Page 173
Magic squares

12	6	3	13
7	9	16	2
14	4	5	11
1	15	10	8

16	3	2	13
5	10	11	8
9	6	7	12
4	15	14	1

Here are two configurations. Have you found any others?

Page 174
Mega numbers
Circle puzzle
Join 1 to 7 and 4 to 10.

Page 175
Fill it in
$5 + 6 - 3 = 8$
$5 \times 3 - 6 = 9$
$(5 - 3) \times 6 = 12$
$5 + 3 + 6 = 14$
$5 \times 3 \times 4 = 90$

Page 176
Puzzle it out

	3 litre container now holds	5 litre container now holds
1. Fill the 3 litre container.	3 litres	0 litres
2. Pour those three litres into the 5 litre container.	0 litres	3 litres
3. Fill the 3 litre container again	3 litres	3 litres
4. Fill the 5 litre container from the 3 litre container. 1 litre will remain in the smaller container.	1 litre	5 litres
5. Empty the 5 litre container.	1 litre	0 litres
6. Pour the water from the small container into the 5 litre container	0 litres	1 litre
7. Fill the 3 litre container again.	3 litres	1 litre
8. Pour the water from the small container into the 5 litre container.	0 litres	4 litres

Page 182

Pantomime Puzzle
ANSWERS:
1. BILLY CONNOLLY
2. BRUCE FORSYTHE
3. VICTORIA WOOD
4. TONY BLACKBURN
5. JASON DONOVAN
6. PHILLIP SCHOFIELD
7. UNA STUBBS
8. FRANK BRUNO
9. PAMELA STEVENSON
10. JASPER CARROTT

Page 184
Disc dilemma

Page 185
Brainteasers
1. Nine – both parents, five boys and just two girls.
2. If it's legal for a dead man to marry!

Page 186
Me and my shadow!
Figure 1 with shadow 2

Figure 2 with shadow 4
Figure 3 with shadow 1
Figure 4 with shadow 3

Page 188
Odd socks
Three. Even if she chooses one pink sock and one blue sock, the third one MUST make a pair with one or the other.

Page 189
Mystery eggs Ducks!

Page 191
Mega travel (Do you know ...)
1. Chinese
2. Mount Everest
3. The Amazon River
4. Lake Baikal, Siberia
5. Mexico City, Mexico
6. The Pacific Ocean

Page 193
World trip
a) Amsterdam
b) New York
c) Moscow
d) Cape Town
e) Peking
f) London

Page 194
Mega travel
Flag puzzle
a) Sweden
b) Canada
c) Argentina
d) Scotland
e) Estonia
f) New Zealand

Page 196

Foreign stamps

1. Finland
2. Belgium
3. Spain
4. The Netherlands (Holland)
5. Poland
6. Iceland
7. Italy
8. France
9. Norway
10. Switzerland

Page 199

Time shattering

Page 200

Brainteaser

E (It's a series of the first letters of counting numbers: *O*ne *T*wo *T*hree *F*our *F*ive *S*ix *S*even *E*ight...

Page 201

Maze

Page 203

Brainteasers

1. Hold the egg 2 metres above the pavement. Let it drop 1 metre, and then catch it!
2. QUEUE

Page 206

Army puzzle

1. Private
2. Corporal
3. Sergeant
4. Warrant Officer
5. Lieutenant
6. Captain
7. Major
8. Colonel
9. Brigadier
10. General

Page 208

Mega-brain quiz

1. The Sahara Desert
2. Olive Oyl
3. Yuri Gagarin
4. King Midas
5. They eat aphids (green flies).
6. George Washington
7. Athens, Greece
8. Twenty-six
9. Persia
10. It is red
11. A kind of cattle
12. Because it is lighter than the air we breathe, so it makes balloons float.
13. Mars
14. An igloo
15. Judas Iscariot
16. Indian and African
17. Elvis Presley
18. Canada
19. John Lennon, Paul McCartney, George Harrison, Ringo Starr (Richard Starkey)
20. Siam
21. South America
22. 7:00 am.
23. Cave-dweller
24. Michaelangelo
25. Water

Page 210
Mega sports Crossword

Across:
1. Test matches
7. Elevens
8. Netball
9. Umpires
13. Trampolines

Down:
1. Tennis Court

2. Side
3. Mile
4. Time
5. Hops
6. Substitutes
9. UEFA
10. Prop
11. Real
12. Spin

Page 212
Mega sports

England won the gold medal, USA the silver, and France the bronze.

Page 214
With which sport . . .

1. Decathlon
2. Cricket
3. Tennis
4. Athletics
5. Swimming
6. Motor Racing
7. Golf
8. Snooker
9. Tennis
10. Football

Page 215
Football muddle

1. West Ham
2. Crystal Palace
3. Nottingham Forest
4. Aston Villa
5. Plymouth Argyle
6. Sheffield Wednesday
7. Manchester United
8. Leyton Orient
9. Tottenham Hotspur
10. Bristol Rovers

Page 216
Olympigram

(a) Helsinki (1952)
(b) Montreal (1976)
(c) Mexico City (1968)
(d) Los Angeles (1984)
(e) Moscow (1980)

Page 217
Brainteaser

A melted snowman's eyes and nose

Page 218
Picture puzzle

1. Mole
2. Earring
3. Pattern on waistband
4. Pattern on ribbon
5. Design on sleeve

Page 220
Matchstick puzzles
Puzzle 1

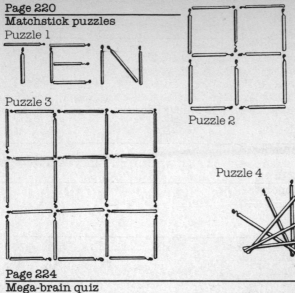

Puzzle 3

Puzzle 2

Puzzle 4

Page 224
Mega-brain quiz
Answers:
1. A Very Important Person
2. Charles Dickens
3. Jupiter
4. Troy
5. A vixen
6. Vincent van Gogh
7. Seoul
8. Leonardo da Vinci
9. From one of Adam's ribs
10. Pompeii
11. The Vatican City, in Rome, Italy
12. 'The Queen of Hearts, she made some *tarts*...'
13. The Golden Fleece
14. Hebrew
15. A kind of butterfly

Page 226
Mega words Watch your spelling
1. a) key
   b) quay
2. a) boy
   b) buoy
3. a) root
   b) route
4. a) leak
   b) leek
5. a) pair
   b) pear
6. a) bear
   b) bare
7. a) mail
   b) male
8. a) mussels
   b) muscles

Page 228
Mix-up
Silly verse
Won-one was a racehorse;
Tutu was one, too.
Won-one won one race one day;
Tutu won one, too!

1. A choir of angels
2. A flock of sheep
3. A class of schoolchildren
4. A stampede of cattle
5. A swarm of insects
6. An army of soldiers
7. A team of footballers
8. A gaggle of Geese

Page 229
Mega words Word study
Astronomy is the study of the universe.
Radiology is the study of X-ray radiation.
Graphology is the study of handwriting.
Astrology is the study of how the stars affect human beings.
Philately is the study of postage stamps.

Page 230
Do you know?
Here are the ones we thought of. Can you think of any more?

1. FACETIOUS, ABSTEMIOUS
2. a) TRICKSTER
   b) LIGHTNESS
   c) PATCHWORK
   d) MATCHSTICK

Page 231
Palindrome puzzle
a) Shahs
b) Repaper
c) Solos
d) Sagas
e) Nun

Page 232
Old Mr Mullens's son

Page 234
Shopping list
1. Bread
2. Fish
3. Potatoes
4. Cakes
5. Meat
6. Biscuits

Page 237
Thin writing   MINI   WIN   MAIN

Page 240
1. SOS (which is short for 'Save Our Souls' – which means HELP!)
2. POLICE
3. FIRE
4. BANANAS!

Page 242
Navy lark
1. Able Seaman
2. Fleet Chief Petty Officer
3. Midshipman
4. Sub Lieutenant
5. Lieutenant
6. Lieutenant Commander
7. Commander
8. Captain
9. Admiral

Page 243
Puzzle picture
Numbers 2 and 6: these two have three dots; all the others, two.

Page 244

Books and authors

a) 3   c) 4   e) 5
b) 1   d) 6   f) 2

Page 246

Mega-brain quiz

1. The Wind in the Willows
2. Mercury
3. Woodstock
4. A pentagon
5. Blue, white, and red
6. Under the Arc de Triomphe
7. Deliberately setting fire to property
8. The peseta
9. Peter Tchaikovsky
10. Stratford-upon-Avon
11. 98.4°F or about 37°C
12. A raised alphabet that the blind can read
13. The river Tiber
14. Alexander Graham Bell
15. The Taj Mahal
16. Paris
17. The game of badminton
18. Indigo

Page 248

Occupational hazard

1. Violinist (musician): b)
2. Gardener: f)
3. Ballerina: a)
4. Tailor or seamstress: g)
5. Teacher: d)
6. Blacksmith: h)
7. Artist: e)
8. Hairdresser: c)

Page 250

Mega creatures

Across:
1. POLAR BEAR
6. NOSES
8. GUPPY
12. DALMATIAN

Down:
1. PUSS
2. LION
3. RATS
4. EELS
5. ROOK
7. COLD
8. GULL
9. PUMA
10. YETI
11. SWAN

Page 252
Beastly puzzle
PHELANTE = ELEPHANT
LUVREUT = VULTURE
NOLI = LION
ANSEKS = SNAKES

HOPIP = HIPPO
DICCOROLE = CROCODILE
RETGI = TIGER

Page 256
Rings before the eyes 18

Page 257
Sinking feeling
13 days. By the end of the 12th day he will have climbed 12 metres. On the 13th day, he'll climb three metres to the top!

Page 260 Mega illusion They are the same length!

Page 262
Brain teasers
1. None – it's a PEAR tree!
2. Big John's two mates go first. One returns by himself and gives the boat to Big John, who rows over. He gets out and the other mate crosses again to retrieve his friend.

Page 263
Triangle tease 26

Page 264
Figure it out 6

Page 266
Picture puzzle
fish – dish

pie – fly
egg – peg
man – fan
mat – hat

spoon – moon
saw – paw
peas – keys
heart – tart
dots – knots

Page 268
Mega-brain quiz
1. The Prime Minister of the U.K.
2. Lewis Carroll
3. A noisy ghost
4. Warsaw
5. Sherwood Forest, Nottingham
6. St Christopher
7. The pyramids of Egypt
8. Sturgeon roe (eggs)
9. Reginald Dwight
10. Mars
11. The lira
12. Moscow
13. Gondolas
14. Sputnik I
15. Spanish
16. The Andes (in South America)
17. Shere Khan
18. Tennis

Page 270
Perception puzzle
'the' has been written twice

Page 271
Spot the film
RAIDERS OF THE LOST ARK
SUPERMAN
STAR WARS
GHOST BUSTERS
BAMBI
JAWS
THE WIZARD OF OZ
THE JUNGLE BOOK
E.T.
MARY POPPINS

Page 272
Mega-pop Crossword

Across:
  1. DOORS
  5. STATUS
  6. REM
  7. MINDS
  8. ELVIS
 10. SPROUT

Down:
  2. MADNESS
  3. BEATLES
  4. ROSES (See 9 down)
  7. MICK
  9. GUNS (See 4 down)

Page 274
  1. ELVIS PRESLEY
  2. ROLLING STONES
  3. BEE GEES
  4. KYLIE MINOGUE
  5. MICHAEL JACKSON
  6. SINEAD O'CONNOR
  7. PHIL COLLINS
  8. SIMPLY RED
  9. GEORGE MICHAEL
 10. JIMI HENDRIX